The Model

The Model

37 Years Investing in Asian Equities

By Richard H. Lawrence, Jr., CFA
with James E. Hackett

Contributions by:
James Squire
Leonie Foong
William Leung

HARRIMAN HOUSE LTD

Email: enquiries@harriman-house.com
Website: harriman.house

First published 2021. Second printing 2024.
Copyright © Overlook Investments Limited.

The right of Richard H. Lawrence, Jr., James Squire, Leonie Foong and William Leung to be identified as the Authors has been asserted in accordance with the Copyright, Design and Patents Act 1988.

Hardback ISBN: 978-0-85719-959-1

高觀授資

For Dee,
my partner in life who has been
my North Star and best friend for the
entirety of Overlook's journey.

Contents

The
Overlook
Model

*Buy some stocks and wait for them to go up, and then sell
them. If they don't go up, don't buy them.*

— WILL ROGERS,
American humorist and social commentator

OVID AND MY wife, Dee, gave me the time to write this book.
I had no trips to Asia, no trips to see Overlook's investors, no
trips to attend board meetings for the National Audubon
Society. And Dee had the patience to listen to the wandering thoughts of
a first-time author.

The book is a celebration of Overlook's three decades. It is a modest gift to
what we call the Overlook Community: all the investors that have allocated
long-term capital to Overlook and permitted us to follow our passion of
investing in one of the most interesting parts of the world. My gratitude
extends to all the colleagues, executives, advisors and friends who have
supported Overlook these past decades.

I am proud to say that it is also the book that I wish I could have read when I was in my 30s and was searching to put together all the pieces of The Overlook Model.

The goal of the book is to answer two simple questions:

1. How did Overlook achieve its success?

2. How can Overlook best ensure future success?

We grew at 14.3% for three decades. We outperformed the universe by 6.5 percentage points per year for 30 years. More importantly, we delivered 14.2% returns to the Overlook investors. We outperformed when we were a small fund, we outperformed when we were a mid-sized fund, and we continue to outperform as a large fund. We outperformed when I made every stock pick and we have continued to outperform now that I make almost none of the stock picks.

The only logical and believable explanation is that the success was generated by the consistent execution of The Overlook Model, and this gives us confidence about the future.

This book will describe The Overlook Model with a level of detail never before disclosed. Most members of the Overlook Community will instantly recognize the depiction of the Model with its six interlocking components. However, few members of the Overlook Community will know all the stories, experiences, people, companies, hard lessons and joyful moments that allowed the Model to become The Model.

Map of The Model

We have structured this book in five parts:

I.   *Bear Markets*: We tell the story of Overlook's experiences in the 1997/98 Asian Crisis, when Asia came close to complete economic collapse. In the latter chapter of Part One, we discuss essential lessons on how to survive bear markets.

II.   *The Overlook Model*: We describe the Overlook Investment Philosophy and how we deliver results through the Overlook Business Practices. We will explain for the first time how a Margin of Safety can be achieved, both for investors and for companies.

III.   *Overlook in China*: We describe Overlook's journey from chasing rainbows in the 1980s to investing in some of the most compelling companies in the world in recent years.

IV.   *The Voices of Overlook*: Each of the four members of Overlook's Investment Committee share their views on important investment topics.

V.   *The Poster Child*: We follow the unique story of Overlook's 20-year investment in Asia's finest public company: Taiwan Semiconductor Manufacturing Company.

How We Tell the Overlook Story

There are four components of our effort to bring the story of Overlook to life.

First, we have included stories of companies, executives, people and events. Life is really a series of stories, and stories are what bring richness to our lives. My Partners and I describe a few successes, but the failures had a disproportionally large impact on the creation of The Overlook Model and so we have shared stories of the failures too. The hard lessons learned and stories of stock picks gone bad are interspersed with descriptions of what we call Asia's New Winners – some of the great companies that Overlook has invested in over the past three decades.

Second, I hope *The Model* will be taken as a moderately serious investment book. I love few things in life as much as a great investment book. They have been major contributors to our professional lives and to Overlook's success as an investor. Books and relationships allowed us to identify Overlook's cousins: Richard H. Lawrence, Sr., Jonathan Bush, Benjamin Graham, Peter Lynch, Warren Buffett, Marc Faber, John Train, Leon Levy, David Swensen, John Neff, Jack Bogle, Jeremy Grantham, the Outstanding Investors Digest (OID) newsletter, The CFA's *Classics: An Investor's Anthology,* Volumes 1–3, and the third edition of *Investment Analysis and Portfolio Management* by Cohen, Zinbarg and Zeikel, which introduced me to the DuPont Model. And the list goes on. Overlook is proud to be at least a distant cousin to these giants.

These cousins, and many more, accelerated our learning experiences and gave us the ability to extract nuggets of wisdom that ended up contributing to The Model. The way my dad and Jon Bush controlled their assets under management surely had an impact on our establishing the legal Cap on Subscriptions that we utilize at Overlook. The way Marc Faber wrote about bear markets impacted how we operate in tough times. The way John Neff thought about portfolio construction has stayed with us for nearly three decades. Importantly for Overlook, the way OID presented incredibly detailed company analyses showed me the level of detail that I needed to secure on our holdings. You get the idea.

I have no expectation that I have written a great investment book, but I hope the descriptions of the Overlook Investment Philosophy and Business Practices, Asia's New Winners, the Art of Selling, and a few of the hard lessons we have learned, might help current and future generations of investment professionals add a nugget or two into their own models.

Third, I am thrilled that *The Model* has given me a platform to acknowledge the contributions of outstanding Asian executives. So many Asian executives have managed their businesses brilliantly and it has been just so much fun to work alongside them. As a group, I have huge respect for the modern Asian executive. Sure, there are alpha males and greedy executives who I try to avoid; however, on balance, the Asian CEO is instinctive and intelligent, but also strategic and long term. I said for a long time that successful corporate leadership is a genetic trait, but I have come to realize over the past decades that it is a skill built from the ground up through hard work. It is no surprise to Overlook that Asia has cultivated so many New Winners.

Fourth, throughout this book, we will use excerpts from Overlook quarterly reports which relate directly to the topics being discussed and which were written as events occurred. We intend that these real-time reports provide an accurate historical perspective and an immediacy of insight that only first-hand accounts can give. In some cases we have modestly edited the excerpts for clarity, but in each case we have maintained the original intent.

The Overlook Executive Team

To tell the Overlook story, we must introduce you to the Overlook executive team. These are the people who make it all happen. We are a small, focused team of talented and dedicated individuals who have demonstrated the ability to execute The Model successfully. The senior members of the Overlook executive team include:

James Squire, Partner and Chief Investment Officer

Leonie Foong, Partner

William Leung, Partner

Alan Morgan, Partner and Chief Operating Officer

The people at Overlook came together over the years because we had read many of the same investment books, studied the same great investors, and been drawn to the same companies. We understand that The Overlook

Model provides a platform to collectively achieve greater success than we could on our own. We all agree that fundamental company analysis is essential to inform our investment decisions. And we all share an appreciation for working together to invest correctly across Asia.

Our effectiveness as a team, however, should not mask the incredible diversity of personalities, experiences and strengths that each individual brings to Overlook. Our work together is stimulating, interesting and challenging. We all contribute, debate, listen, and respect each other. This book is not about "I"; it is about "We." It is true that I founded Overlook in 1991 and pieced together the core components of The Overlook Model, but the execution of The Model, and the successes we have achieved, are all "We."

Lessons Learned

Surprisingly, writing the book taught us a few things about Overlook's three-decade history in the investment management business which we sort of knew but did not fully appreciate:

- Mistakes are times of critical learning.

- Hong Kong has provided us the perfect home.

- Bear markets are essential times when we must show our mettle. You can't swing and miss in a bear market.

- Asia's New Winners emerged from the 1997/98 Asian Crisis, the 2007/08 Global Financial Crisis and the 2007/13 China Bear Market and contributed outsized gains for Overlook. It is a tribute to Asia's corporate leadership that New Winners just keep appearing out of the wreckage.

- Long duration is the name of the game. Short-term success is nice, but Overlook's three-decade history is what all of us at Overlook are most proud of.

- We defined for the first time the Overlook Margin of Safety, a concept that had eluded me for over four decades in the investment management business.

- And we made a connection that successful companies, like successful asset managers, must achieve excellence of performance, but must also deliver that performance to shareholders with effective business practices.

Hong Kong, Our Home

I arrived in Hong Kong in 1985 at what turned out to be the most transformative period in Asia's history. I often say I would rather be lucky than smart, and in Hong Kong in 1985 I got lucky beyond my wildest dreams. The city at that time was the entrepreneur's hangout; it was the place I had unknowingly been searching for my entire life.

The Joint Declaration had been signed 15 months earlier, and while many Hong Kongers took the return of Hong Kong to China as a reason to move to Vancouver, I took it as a sign that Hong Kong was the most exciting place to be.

Deng Xiaoping had asserted power and was moving China 180 degrees in a different direction. We watched first-hand as Deng became one of Overlook's most respected leaders of the past century.

The Special Economic Zones were being established, signaling China was changing in ways and at a speed that was hard to fathom. And the Hong Kong entrepreneurs were opening China's doors to the rest of the world.

The book begins at its natural starting point: June 30, 1997, the day of the Handover of Hong Kong back to China. Dee and I hosted, with friends, a party at our apartment on the Peak on a night of just brutal rain. We celebrated the successes of the British and we anxiously awaited the arrival of China.

Of course, little did I know that two days later the Thai baht would devalue and life would be turned upside down in ways that I had never experienced and certainly had not prepared for. The 1997/98 Asian Crisis was about to leave the starting gate.

PART ONE

Bear Markets

Life is lived forward, but understood backwards.

— SOREN KIERKEGAARD,
Danish existentialist philosopher

IN THE EARLY 1990s, Asia was enjoying a remarkable period of growth and prosperity. Stock markets were rising, property markets were rocketing, business investment and manufacturing exports were climbing.

But the rapid growth also strained Asian financial systems. By the mid-1990s, imbalances began to emerge. There was now too much unhedged dollar debt, excessive capacity, and ballooning current account deficits. The laws of economics have limited patience for such imbalances; and when the necessary reforms were too slow in coming, crisis became inevitable. When the crisis hit on July 2, 1997, in what became known as the 1997/98 Asian Crisis, it was nothing less than an economic nightmare.

The first chapter in Part One is the story of Overlook's experiences through that 1997/98 Asian Crisis. We tell the story chronologically, with the relentless drumbeat of bad news and panic seen in real-time reports, as written by Overlook from quarter to quarter. We will begin in the calm before the storm, in June 1997, when most of us were focused on the Handover of Hong Kong from Britain to China which would take place on the 30th of the month.

The story of the 1997/98 Asian Crisis is also a story of bear markets: how trouble brings change, how the weak get flushed, and how New Winners emerge.

In the second chapter of Part One, we move on to look at the lessons we have learned from investing during bear markets.

Voracious!
The 1997/98 Asian Crisis

I have never read of, or seen, such a total economic breakdown and massive destruction of wealth as has occurred, against all expectations, in Asia in the last six months.

— MARC FABER,
Author, *The Gloom, Boom & Doom Report*,
February 12, 1998

When We Still Slept at Night

THE GOOD NEWS

In June 1997, it all seemed perfect. I had founded Overlook six years earlier. I was living in Hong Kong happily with my wife and two young kids, doing what I had always wanted to do: picking stocks in Asia.

Overlook was keeping its head above water in a bear market, or what we thought was *the* bear market. In 1996, markets in Thailand were down 36.8%; Korea was down 32.8%. Overlook, however, finished the year up 7.9%.

In the first half of 1997, Thailand dropped another 34.7%; but Overlook finished the first half of 1997 up 6.4%, and up 282.7% since inception.

We still slept at night. We did our homework at Overlook, ran all the analyses, made all the company visits, and concluded that our companies were profitable, growing, and strong.

Famous last words: I reported to Overlook's investors that in the coming months, "staying the course should reward us as investors."

THE BAD NEWS

I should have known better.

Warren Buffett had been quoted in the financial press as saying that investors didn't need to worry about economic conditions; they only had to concern themselves with the strength and prospects of individual companies. I am sorry I ever read that article.

The warning signs were there in plain sight. I was an economics major in college and considered myself at least reasonably well informed about macroeconomic trends. I recognized the economic excesses and imbalances in Asia, but... See previous paragraph.

We determined a geographic allocation of the portfolio, including: Thailand, 29.3%; Indonesia, 28.1%; Korea, 14.5%. We allocated a combined 72% of our portfolio to those three countries. Within a year, all three countries would require emergency funding from the IMF to stay afloat.

We actually thanked ourselves on June 24, 1997, that we had not hedged our currency positions. That was wrong—laughably wrong.

June 24, 1997: On the Brink

▼ OVERLOOK PERFORMANCE:
DOWN 1.1% FROM PEAK

The following quarterly report was sent to Overlook's investors on June 24, 1997, in which we describe the mounting pressures on Asian economies and companies.

I feel a sense of déjà vu as I write this letter to you and feel compelled, yet again, to comment on the events in Thailand. Economists, analysts, fund managers, and journalists are unanimous in their attacks on Thailand, predicting depression, massive devaluation, surging non-performing loans, political incompetence, and gross economic mismanagement. In all my years, I have never seen such a one-way market, and I can only conclude that they do not own our stocks.

Thailand's problems revolve around the high current account deficit, past overinvestment in many non-productive assets such as Bangkok property, rising non-performing loans triggered by lax supervision of finance companies, and a mathematically fixed currency rate. There are solutions to all of these problems, although they are emerging too slowly for fund managers and analysts. Frankly, the Government has done a poor job in maintaining confidence, and that has caused the problems to snowball with each decline in the stock market.

To bail out of Overlook's investments after such a stock market decline seems nonsensical to us, so we hunker down, monitor our businesses closely, and thank ourselves that we do not own any leveraged property companies or under-reserved finance companies, and that we have not hedged our currency position to date.

HOW DID IT GET SO BAD SO QUICKLY?

Following that report, on July 2, with the suddenness of a stakes race at Happy Valley Racecourse, the collapse of Asian currencies started with the devaluation of the Thai baht, then rapidly spread like a pandemic to currencies across the region. The crisis had officially begun.

The collapse of confidence that accompanied the crashing currencies poured fuel on the fire. Foreign capital, the so-called "hot money," was withdrawn from Asia in a panic, crushing share prices, which exerted even more downward pressure on currencies and upward pressure on interest rates.

For Overlook, there was just nowhere to hide. That was bad enough, but the economic collapse also exposed a devastating weakness in the Asian financial system that we call the Bankruptcy Bomb.

ASIA'S BANKRUPTCY BOMB

Throughout the early 1990s, many companies in Asia took loans in U.S. dollars because interest rates on dollar debt were so much lower. With stable currencies, it was a sensible idea.

For example, in January 1995, a company might borrow US$ 100 million at 8% when lending rates in Thailand were near 14%. As long as the exchange rate of the Thai baht remained fixed at 25:1 to the U.S. dollar, there was little risk and the company enjoyed substantial interest savings. Good move. Most companies did not hedge the currency exposure which would have negated the interest rate advantage.

However, when the value of the Thai baht fell from 25:1 to 50:1 to the U.S. dollar, that US$ 100 million loan, when measured in local currency, increased from baht 2,500 million to baht 5,000 million. In other words, the company now needed to earn twice as much in Thai baht to service the same U.S. dollar loan. In countless cases, bankruptcy followed. Thus, the widespread use of unhedged U.S. dollar debt had become a Bankruptcy Bomb for companies and, by extension, for entire economies.

No investor exposed to unhedged dollar debt could remain unaffected by the currency crisis, but to Overlook's modest credit we were aware of the dangers and had no direct exposure to any company that exploited the practice. We preferred companies with low debt, that had the high cash flow and high earnings to finance growth internally: those with, as we like to say, "bombproof balance sheets." BBL Dharmala was one such company.

LARCENY, AND A BANKRUPTCY BOMB IN JAKARTA

In June 1997 we wrote to Overlook's investors about our investment in BBL Dharmala, which provided purchase financing for heavy equipment, commercial vehicles, and passenger cars in Indonesia. We were familiar with the industry, having invested successfully in niche finance companies throughout Asia since 1992.

BBL Dharmala ticked all the boxes. It was a well-managed company. We had owned its shares for four years and in that time E.P.S. had compounded at 33.4%, with an average interest rate spread in its loan portfolio of 6.9%. We liked that Bangkok Bank, the largest private bank in Thailand, was a joint venture partner at BBL Dharmala, as this gave us some comfort on matters of corporate governance. Importantly, BBL Dharmala's U.S. dollar debt was fully hedged. We bought the stock at a bargain value, and we considered BBL Dharmala an intelligent investment with potential to remain a long-term hold in the portfolio.

WHAT COULD GO WRONG?

In June 1997, the Indonesian rupiah traded at a value of about 2,500 to the U.S. dollar. Seven months later, in January 1998, the value of the rupiah had fallen to nearly 10,000 to the dollar, a mind-bending decline. No worries for BBL Dharmala, we thought, because its U.S. dollar debt, as mentioned, was fully hedged.

WHAT DID GO WRONG?

The Gondokusumo family, who owned the controlling stake in BBL Dharmala, appropriated the currency hedge. That's correct: in January 1998, the Gondokusumo family simply transferred the hedge from BBL Dharmala to protect their personal interests. It was wrong, but under Indonesian law we had little recourse. We enlisted the help of Bangkok Bank, which was then fighting its own close encounter with death in Thailand, to no avail. The $100 million currency hedge was worth more to the family than their partial ownership of BBL Dharmala shares, so they sacrificed the company and its shareholders, took the hedge, and got away with it. Dystopian greed had entered the bear market culture.

Without the currency hedge, BBL Dharmala was immediately bankrupt. We sold our shares for pennies on the dollar, generating an IRR of −57.4% over six years. No one from the Gondokusumo family ever went to jail.

September 1997: Surreal Madness

▼ OVERLOOK PERFORMANCE:
DOWN 25.4% FROM PEAK

Q3 1997: NEWS FROM THE WAR ZONE

July 2, 1997: Thailand devalues the baht, which falls 20% in one day. Other Asian currencies begin to falter.

July 24, 1997: Currency jitters turn to panic. Meltdown sweeps Asia.

August 14, 1997: Asian stock markets plunge. Everyone runs for the exits.

> **September 4, 1997:** Philippine peso falls to record low. Malaysian Prime Minister Mahathir bin Mohamad vows to combat foreign speculators with a US$ 20 billion initiative to support the stock market. It doesn't work.

A 25.4% decline from peak is hard to defend. But what was it really like in Asia in September 1997? A picture is worth a thousand words. Think: Edvard Munch's *The Scream.*

In times of panic, we grasp for calm. Only now can I laugh at the self-calming understatement of two sentences I used in our September 1997 report:

> "Conditions for equity investors in Asia remain extremely difficult."

> "We are convinced that our companies will survive; they have the balance sheets and cash flows to survive; and, so far, their businesses have shown great resilience."

One must read between those lines to see the 16-hour days, the sleepless nights, the unrelenting bad news, and the sheer voraciousness of the fall.

In the same September 1997 report, we also reviewed Multi Bintang, a great company in our portfolio whose story of survival reflects the surreal madness of those times.

CHEERS, MULTI BINTANG

I first came across Multi Bintang in 1985 as my wife and I were walking along a beach in Bali. We passed a young man raking the beach who wore a distinctive hat with a Bir Bintang logo. In the hot equatorial sun he wore no shirt; and I wore no hat, having recently lost mine during our travels. I approached the man and offered him literally the shirt off my back for his hat. He gladly exchanged his Indonesian Bir Bintang hat for my American Pep Boys T-shirt. Little could I have imagined that eight years later Overlook would own 2% of the company.

In September 1997, we wrote the following:

> Multi Bintang (MBL) is the dominant beer producer in Indonesia, owned and operated by Heineken N.V. of Holland. MBL currently has over 80% market share in what is a growing and profitable beer market. MBL has generated a superior long-term track record in growth and profitability. From 1987 to 1996, sales and net profits grew at a compound rate of 20.6% and 22.3%, respectively. Over the same period the return on equity averaged 34.8%, which allowed MBL to maintain an average dividend payout ratio of 73% and keep its debt level modest.
>
> Throughout all the disruption in Southeast Asia, the tendency to misunderstand the details, both positive and negative, presents opportunities for Overlook. We are attracted by Heineken's savvy management, MBL's bombproof balance sheet, Indonesia's tiny per capita consumption of beer, and the company's past record of growing profits in U.S. dollar terms. The stock sells at just over 10 times earnings, with a 5.0% yield, and with 20% compound growth target intact for the company. If MBL sells off, we will look to increase our holding.

The story does not end there.

A BAD OMEN IN JAKARTA

For all of Multi Bintang's strengths and resilience, we were increasingly aghast at the economic outlook in Indonesia. Events were deteriorating so quickly that the economic news was out of date by the time it was released. I had to see the situation for myself, so I scheduled a trip to visit all of our Indonesian companies.

I stayed at the Hilton Hotel in Jakarta because it was conveniently located near one of the greatest cloverleaf intersections of all time; but also, after a long day of meetings, I could play tennis. One evening, thoroughly sweaty from the exercise and the humidity, I crossed the hotel's outdoor patio and noticed a group of people closely inspecting items spread out on the ground. Only one man was speaking, pointing to the items as the others listened and nodded. Curious, I slowed down to get a peek.

There were automatic rifles and handguns laid out in plain view. The man speaking was clearly an arms dealer, plying his goods in the Hilton Hotel. Shaken, I kept moving. This was bad, very bad. This was a bad omen for Indonesia.

No matter how strong the fortifications corrupt dictators erect to protect their power, economics will ultimately prove to be their Achilles heel. In Indonesia, the economic devastation was particularly harsh. The currency collapsed. Stock markets crashed. Interest rates rose to 99% and could not go higher due to the IT system of banks that prevented the rate from expanding to three digits. Mass unemployment brought the people to the brink. President Suharto, 32 years in office, barely clung to power. Civil unrest smoldered until, in May 1998, the unrest exploded in riots across Indonesia.

In Tangerang, an industrial suburb of Jakarta where Multi Bintang's facilities were located, rioters threw rocks, broke windows, burned buildings and looted stores. At Multi Bintang's facilities, the office building in the front of the property was completely trashed. Fortunately, all Multi Bintang employees had escaped to the undamaged brewery building on the rear of the property. No one at Multi Bintang was hurt.

The Multi Bintang story eventually reached a successful conclusion. President Suharto was forced from office by popular revolt on May 21, 1998. Indonesia eventually recovered to economic health. Multi Bintang was uniquely well situated to survive 97/98, having lived through other close encounters in Indonesia over the prior 80 years. The company continued to grow and prosper. It remained in Overlook's portfolio for many years and became the successful long-term investment we had always known it could be. We eventually sold our shares after 19.2 years, generating a 19.5% IRR in U.S. dollars.

December 1997: On the Front Lines

▼ OVERLOOK PERFORMANCE:
DOWN 49.1% FROM PEAK

Q4 1997: NEWS FROM THE WAR ZONE

October 23–28, 1997: Hong Kong stock market loses nearly one-quarter of its value in four days on fears over interest rates and downward pressure on Hong Kong dollar; other Asian markets also plunge.

November 7, 1997: South Korea's market falls 7%, its largest single-day decline to date.

November 17, 1997: The Bank of Korea abandons its effort to defend the won, which falls to a record low of 1,000 to the dollar.

November 24, 1997: South Korean stocks fall 7.2% on fears that the IMF may demand tough reforms.

December 8, 1997: The Thai Government announces that it will close 56 insolvent finance companies as part of the IMF's economic restructuring plan. 30,000 white-collar workers lose their jobs.

Marc Faber, an old friend, mentioned in the latest **Gloom, Boom, & Doom Report** *that it requires "courage, enthusiasm, sacrifice, endurance and, at times, risk taking" to reach the goal of building wealth. Certainly, I can confirm the accuracy of his comment and perhaps I would add a few more, such as: a thick skin, a ton of exercise, a sense of humor, an understanding spouse, and dedicated employees. My dad always said you need to be standing at the end of a bear market, and he was right!*

— RICHARD H. LAWRENCE, Jr., December 1997

This is the story from the front lines of the bear market, as told in our December 1997 report:

The simultaneous collapse of the region's capital markets, currencies, and confidence during 1997 exposed critical weaknesses in Asia and triggered a massive decline in the U.S. dollar per capita income for over 380 million people. During 18 years of investing, I have never witnessed such a dramatic and chaotic reversal of business conditions and wealth.

Needless to say, equity investors suffered mightily as the last vestiges of denial by governments and central bankers were swept aside by markets and currencies that would simply not stop going down. The pain is most likely not over, although the declines already discount a great deal of the economic implosion.

The value of the Overlook portfolio declined by a shocking 49.1%, of which 38% represented losses due to currencies and 62% represented losses on equity positions. Thailand and Indonesia were by far the most painful areas for Overlook, contributing 74% of the loss overall, but all markets and all currencies (save for the Hong Kong dollar) had a hand in the decline. Suffice to say we found no place to hide in Asia.

The momentum behind Asia's sell-off has been frankly overwhelming, as demonstrated by Overlook's decline in November and December despite the defensive positions we assumed earlier in the Fall. We see many of our investments being sold by investors who are disregarding values and simply want out, and want out quickly.

As we fight in the trenches to preserve value in the face of the sharp deterioration of economies and businesses, it is easy to disregard the current opportunity that presents itself for all of our partners in Asia. For investors sitting overseas, watching your wealth evaporate in a far-off land, it must be difficult to remain positive about the strengths of Asia and the attractions of investing here as opposed to the Dow Jones, which has effortlessly marched upward.

The following chart is what fleeing a market looks like in graphic form.

Thai Property Sub Index, 1994–1998

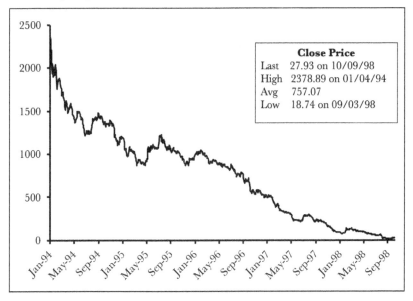

Source: Bloomberg.

The Thai Property Sub Index is down from 2,400 to 30, down 98.7% in local currency and 99.3% in U.S. dollars, and that is a composite index! To give a sense of what a 99.3% decline is like, say you own a stock that goes down 80%, then it drops another 80%. To reach a 99.3% decline, the stock has to drop another 80%. That's three successive declines of 80%!

NIGHT IN HONG KONG, MORNING IN NEW YORK

It would have been nice, in late 1997 and early 1998, if after a long day of bear market madness at the office I could have simply enjoyed an evening relaxing at home with my family. You know, have a beer, talk to my wife, play with my kids, have dinner together, walk the dog, put the kids to bed, read, good night.

But no. With performance down 49.1%, I only got to the point of putting the kids to bed. That would make it about 9:00 PM local time in Hong

Kong, 8:00 AM in New York. It would be another hour before my clients arrived at their offices in New York – when I could call them to explain the situation with Overlook. I would spend that hour girding myself for those phone calls. I can still feel the churning in my stomach, my reluctance to get on the phone, and my dread that, no matter what optimism I could provide, the markets would be down again in the morning.

The rout was on in full force. By the end of December 1997, Overlook had been down by more than 10% per month for five straight months, and this trend would continue through January. I had a family, bills due every month, apartment rent of $13,000 per month (Hong Kong was then one of the most expensive cities in the world), office rent for Overlook, and employees to pay. If Overlook went down, I went down. I needed to make those phone calls. I knew the bear market would eventually end, and I knew that Overlook could succeed. But I needed to convince my clients of that.

"Hi, this is Richard Lawrence calling from Hong Kong."

"Oh, Hong Kong," the surprised assistant would say, as if wondering where Hong Kong is. "I'll put you right through."

To my great disappointment, the calls always went through. I would then ruin the investor's morning with the news from Asia. "Yes, we are down more than 10% again this month. Yes, Korea is about to call in the IMF. Yes, students are protesting across the region. Yes, business conditions are desperate. But did I tell you ThaiRe had another up quarter?"

If even a few of our bigger clients had backed out, Overlook might not have survived. So, I made the calls. The clients grilled me, but they heard me out. Most were more empathetic than angry because they were seasoned investors who had themselves been through bear markets in their careers. It didn't hurt, either, that the S&P 500 Index was up 31% in 1997, offsetting Asia's dismal decline.

But the Bear Market wasn't over yet: how bad could it get?

March 1998: A Future at McDonald's?

▼ OVERLOOK PERFORMANCE:
DOWN 50.6% FROM PEAK

Q1 1998: NEWS FROM THE WAR ZONE

January 8, 1998: The Indonesian rupiah falls to an all-time low.

January 12, 1998: Peregrine Investments files for liquidation. Hang Seng Index plunges.

January 15, 1998: Food prices in Indonesia increase by as much as 80%.

January 22, 1998: Officials from South Korea attempt to restructure the country's short-term debt. The Indonesian rupiah falls to *another* all-time low of 12,000 rupiah against the dollar.

March 24, 1998: Food riots in Indonesia. U.S. sends $70 million in food and medical emergency aid.

In February 1998, Overlook had its first month of positive performance since May 1997. Our relief was muted: despite the single positive month, we remained wary of the lingering economic turmoil. And the Overlook team, after eight long months of punishing declines, was mentally and physically exhausted.

FLIPPING BURGERS OR MAKING FRENCH FRIES

I had no use for being nostalgic for the "good old days" before the Bear Market, nor did I allow myself to be blithely optimistic for better days that may eventually lie ahead. It was all here and now. We had to manage through this crisis, protect the portfolio, defend ourselves as best we could.

It often felt like an unending slog, and the problem was the unavoidable, relentless negativism: we all carried a heavy sack of worries.

There was, however, one person who helped ease the burden of that heavy load: Khun Surachai Sirivallop, CEO of Thai Reinsurance, the leading reinsurance company in Thailand and our largest holding at that time.

It took Overlook a while to recognize the special characteristics of ThaiRe, having bought in 1993 and then sold in January 1994. But by 1996, Overlook had accumulated a 5.4% ownership stake. We wrote: "The potential of ThaiRe began to emerge in 1990 when Khun Surachai became managing director after a successful career at AIA. Under his capable leadership, ThaiRe has emerged as the leading non-life insurance company in Thailand as illustrated by the company's superior track record. Since 1988 net premiums have grown at an annual rate of 26.5%." Khun Surachai was the benevolent king of the Thai insurance industry.

When the Bear Market descended upon Thailand in 1996, then across Asia in 1997, ThaiRe, unlike so many Asian companies, had prepared itself for deteriorating economic conditions. ThaiRe reported net profit growth of 15.4% in 1997, an almost miraculous achievement that capped a six-year stretch when ThaiRe compounded net profits at a rate of 37.3% and did not report a single down quarter. By March 1998, ThaiRe had become the largest holding in the Overlook portfolio. For better or worse, we had hitched our wagon to Khun Surachai, the most capable insurance executive in Asia.

So, when that heavy load of worries seemed almost too much to bear, it was always Khun Surachai and ThaiRe, reporting yet another positive quarter, that helped me to carry on.

Years after the Asian Crisis, I once admitted to Khun Surachai that if ThaiRe had reported a down quarter in 1997/98, I would have thrown in the towel and taken a job flipping burgers at McDonald's in America, to which he replied: "If that had happened, I would be right next to you making the French fries!" Khun Surachai is a fine gentleman, a talented executive, and a member of the Overlook Hall of Fame, which recognizes the best corporate executives we have known.

ThaiRe, under Khun Surachai's leadership, is among the most respected and loved companies Overlook has owned. It remained in our portfolio for 22 years, the pioneer member of the Overlook Two Decade Club of investments we have held for 20 years or more.

MEANWHILE, THE WAR CONTINUED

From our March 1998 report:

> On the back of overseas liquidity and sharply improving current accounts, the Asian stock markets and currencies rallied in the first quarter. Overlook lagged the recovery in part because investors have focused to date on the large cap stocks, and in part because we remain hedged on the currencies and hold cash. If the rallies continue, our portfolio will benefit from broader based buying and the bargain valuations of our major holdings. If the rallies falter in the next few months, the protection on the currencies will provide us with valuable stability.

> 1998 will be a marathon in Asia and we are excited by the prospects for the Overlook portfolio. The portfolio is selling at 5.4 times 1998's estimated E.P.S., with some absolute bargains in the portfolio. We may lag for a period, but as local investors return to the stock markets, I see exciting days ahead.

> Substantial macro threats remain in Asia, including the level of the yen; Indonesia; excess capacity, particularly in property; recapitalization of the banking systems; overheated stock markets in the U.S. and Europe; and China's ongoing struggle with deflation. Problems in any of these areas could cause short-term pain in share prices. We remain leery about chasing stocks in this environment. However, we believe pullbacks will present us with buying opportunities and we have been building a list of targeted stocks that we will buy on future setbacks.

June 1998: Have You Heard Enough?

▼ OVERLOOK PERFORMANCE:
DOWN 59.5% FROM PEAK

Q 2 1 9 9 8 : N E W S F R O M T H E W A R Z O N E

May 5, 1998: Indonesians take to the streets in protest of increasing food and fuel prices, denounce Suharto and demand reform.

May 21, 1998: Indonesia's President Suharto is forced from office after 32 years in power.

May 27, 1998: Russia is on the brink of collapse. Financial markets in Asia and Europe swoon. Hong Kong shares fall 5.3%; Indonesian shares by 3.9%.

May 27–28, 1998: Workers strike in South Korea, where job losses since February have averaged 10,000 per day.

B U T I ' M N O T F I N I S H E D ...

In early June 1998, David Swensen, CIO of the Yale Investment Office, travelled to Asia with his colleague Dean Takahashi and asked for a meeting with me in Hong Kong. Yale was at that time already an investor in Overlook, having suffered the entirety of our 59.5% decline, so I knew David and Dean, and I had dreaded our late-night calls from Hong Kong throughout the bear market.

Due to their travel schedule, the meeting could only occur on a Sunday. It was summer in Hong Kong and I remember being peeved that I would have to pay for air conditioning on a weekend. Bear market thriftiness, perhaps—or was it my wife's concern over the next rent payment?

For our meeting I had prepared a detailed list of what I saw as the risks of investing in Asia after nearly a year of this voracious bear market. I went through one risk after another, explaining how Overlook was managing the portfolio for each one. After about 20 or 25 minutes, David turned to Dean and said, "Dean, have you heard enough?" "Yes." I raised my hand, held up my index finger and said, "But I'm not finished yet." If Yale was going to redeem, well, I at least wanted to have my full say.

Politely, my guests allowed me to continue. When I ran out of gas, David said, "Thank you, Richard, very interesting, but actually we came here today to let you know that we'd like to put another $30 million into Overlook."

Yale's additional investment arrived in September. For the first time in 11 months, I knew that I could pay the kids' education bills and that Overlook would survive. But we were not out of the woods yet.

In the June 1998 letter to Overlook investors, we offered a glimpse of the first light at the end of a very long tunnel:

ASIA'S REFORM AGENDA: CHANGE

The commitment to change is gaining momentum throughout Asia like never before and will serve to underpin another Asian bull market, eventually. While Asia's willingness to change was painfully absent a year ago, the last six months have seen a broad consensus among Asians that change is critical to Asia's very survival, let alone its future growth. Importantly—even critically, from my perspective—governments and Asian citizens have chosen the correct path toward change with an emphasis on freeing up, opening up, and enhancing the market economy.

Specifically, we point to the following areas of change that are ongoing in almost every Asian country, albeit in differing degrees of intensity and effectiveness.

» Political reform is aimed at strengthening transparency, democratic governance, honest elections and bureaucratic accountability.

» Tighter supervision of banks will limit the concentration of risk and loan exposure to non-productive sectors of the economy, like property.

» Stricter provisioning rules on non-performing loans are forcing bank shareholders to recap or face nationalization.

» Wider foreign ownership limits and fewer protected industries will attract foreign investors into Asia.

» Renewed focus of governments on privatization of state-owned assets will rebuild governments' balance sheets.

» Freer labor laws supported by a safety net for unemployed workers will allow corporates to restructure efficiently.

I think it is worth acknowledging that this list of changes goes against strong temptations of politicians to bail out cronies, print money, raise taxes or crack down on political dissent as an answer to social and economic problems. While progress is never achieved in a straight line, it is important that the agenda for change is correctly focused at last.

THE ECONOMIC BACKDROP TO CHANGE

Unfortunately, this reform is being undertaken against a backdrop of brutally difficult economic conditions. I suggest that Asia is now in an economic depression, which my American Heritage dictionary defines as "a period of drastic decline in national or international economy, characterized by decreasing business, falling prices and unemployment." The following phrases form part of our day-to-day vocabulary: negative terms of trade; asset deflation; liquidity trap; consumption collapse; stress tests; and Z-score, an equation that measures a company's likelihood of bankruptcy. Indeed, these are troubling words that reflect the dramatic collapse in Asia throughout the past 12 months.

WHAT WILL THE LONG-TERM FUTURE LOOK LIKE?

To say that Asia will not repeat the mistakes of the past for quite a while is an understatement. As 1929 scared my grandparents' generation, and 1973/74 scared many of my dad's generation, watching well-financed, properly managed companies suffer in the past year is a memory that I will not soon forget. It is back to basics for Asia!

I am increasingly confident that the next cycle will bring higher returns on equity in Asia. The list of factors that will drive Asian corporates to improved returns on investment is long.

» Improved profitability from less competition.

» Improved productivity of corporate assets, both fixed assets and working capital.

» Elimination of non-productive assets and investments, e.g., property.

» Improved capital structures.

» Lower debt levels and lower interest costs.

» Lower break-even points from cost control measures.

» Improved communication with shareholders.

» Improved transparency of businesses and financial accounts.

However, the future described above will not be open to all. I expect numerous corporations will spend the bulk of the next cycle restructuring their debt, trimming their labor force, rebuilding their shareholder base, and reorganizing their manufacturing plants. More than ever before, we feel that the winners of the above trends will be those select companies that have irrefutable cash flow positive businesses, and positive net cash on their balance sheet; companies that have natural access to foreign currencies; companies managed by people of proven integrity; and companies that have cast aside the denial and restructured aggressively.

September 1998: Are You Joking?

▼ OVERLOOK PERFORMANCE:
DOWN 62.0% FROM PEAK

Q3 1998: NEWS FROM THE WAR ZONE

It's gone global!

August 4, 1998: The Dow Jones Industrial Average falls by 3.4%.

August 11, 1998: The Russian market collapses.

August 19, 1998: Russia defaults on its sovereign debt. Panic seizes markets worldwide.

August 31, 1998: The Dow Jones Industrial Average plunges 6.4%.

September 4, 1998: Stocks and bonds free-fall in Latin America.

September 11, 1998: Interest rates in Brazil rise to 50%.

September 24, 1998: U.S. and European markets nosedive as hedge fund Long-Term Capital Management fails, endangering some of the world's largest banks.

THE GUNS OF AUGUST: HONG KONG FIGHTS A SPECULATIVE ATTACK

By August 1998, the Asian Financial Crisis had been raging for over a year. The Hang Seng Index (HSI) had fallen by 59% from 16,673 in August 1997 to 7,936 at the beginning of August 1998. To date, all of the currency pegs in Asia had failed: Thailand, Korea, Indonesia, Malaysia, the Philippines. All, except Hong Kong.

The sharks smelled blood and turned their attention to Hong Kong. Speculators, George Soros notably among them, used the "double play," a tactic they had used successfully elsewhere in Asia, by shorting simultaneously the Hong Kong dollar and the Hang Seng Index. Pressure mounted. Interest rates rose. The HSI fell daily, losing over 1,200 points (16%) in the first nine trading days of the month. The smart bet seemed to be that the peg of the Hong Kong dollar to the U.S. dollar – which had been in place since 1983 – would be broken, the HSI would collapse, and the speculators would walk away with billions, leaving Hong Kong in financial ruins.

On Friday, August 14, Hong Kong counterattacked. The Hong Kong Monetary Authority – in a surprise move coordinated by Joseph Yam, head of the HKMA, Donald Tsang, Finance Secretary, and Tung Chee-hwa, Hong Kong's Chief Executive – unleashed a US$ 15 billion intervention to purchase shares of companies in the Hang Seng Index while simultaneously pushing local interest rates up.

The speculators were initially unfazed. Stanley Druckenmiller, an executive with Soros' Quantum Fund, scoffed, "No matter what they do in their market, when they wake up on Monday morning, they're still going to be in a depression."

The speculators just wanted to make money, but Hong Kong was fighting for its economic survival. The HKMA went all in. It was empowered by Hong Kong's war chest of US$ 100 billion in reserves. It also received support from Zhu Rongji, China's economic tzar, and China's US$ 140 billion in reserves. Each day, the Hong Kong Government bought shares and the Hang Seng Index rose. When the intervention ended on August 28, it had risen by almost 1,200 points, or 17.6%. The speculators scattered, losing the battle and their money. Hong Kong had survived. A year later the HSI reached 13,500, and today exceeds 28,000. It was perhaps the most dramatic move against short sellers by a major financial center in modern history.

THREE PROBLEMS FOR OVERLOOK

At the time of the HKMA counterattack, Overlook faced three extraordinary predicaments. First, we were short the Hang Seng Index Futures in an attempt to preserve equity value for our investors. Second, I had returned to Hong Kong from the U.S. literally the day the intervention was initiated by the HKMA, so I was trying to make sense of these huge events through a fog of jet lag. Third, and what really got me beyond annoyed, was that the HKMA, during the counterattack, did not buy a single share of any stock Overlook owned in Hong Kong, which were all non-index stocks. Not a single share. Was this some sort of cruel joke?

But the battle was over and the battle was won, and we all dreamed of better days ahead.

A QUIET CONFIDENCE

As the news headlines worsen, we are developing a quiet confidence about our long-term future in Asia.

— RICHARD H. LAWRENCE, Jr., September 1998

From our September 1998 report:

> I wrote 13 months ago that Asia faced a crisis of confidence and cash flow. At that time the cash flow was decidedly negative, and confidence had received a brutal body blow from the end of the Asian "miracle" and the birth of the "contagion." As I sit to write this report a year later, it is mind boggling how extensively our world has changed. Today we watch the contagion spread around the globe, bringing crises of confidence and cash flow to Greenwich, Moscow, and Sao Paulo. And we listen to world leaders search for appropriate reforms to global capitalism. What a year!
>
> However, as the news headlines worsen around the world, we are developing a quiet confidence about our long-term future in Asia. The empirical and anecdotal evidence increasingly suggests to us

that Asia is implementing proper reform policies and a platform for future growth is being built. The Thai interest rates have declined from over 22% to less than 8%, with a stable currency to boot. Thailand's comprehensive plan to recapitalize the banking system inexorably advances, providing neither a bailout for weak management nor forced suicide for victims of the country's harsh recession.

All over Asia retail shops and restaurants close daily, wringing out the excess capacity and leaving better business for the survivors. Daily headlines in Hong Kong write of employees accepting 20% wage cuts, reflecting that Hong Kong's fixed exchange rate economy is adjusting. Even in Korea we see progress. Korean bank unions have recently agreed to a 32% reduction in jobs, on top of an 18% decline in employment already this year. Economies and industries are restructuring and the momentum is gathering speed. Against this backdrop, investment values have never been cheaper.

Yet our short-term future will remain volatile and challenging, susceptible to shocks. The external environment remains decidedly negative. Post-election Brazil and leveraged financial institutions in the West scare us. No country in Asia with Brazil's headline numbers survived the contagion intact. No financial institution in Asia with leverage like the major U.S. and European banks survived this Asian downturn without a recapitalization. We see no end to the cancerous spread of the contagion towards the West, implying for Asia a continued period of debt repayments and capital outflow.

PAST WINNERS ARE TODAY'S LOSERS...

After a period when stock picking in Asia has been at best a waste of time, we firmly believe that, in the future, stock picking will add value. Company visits to Asia's traditional high-flyers inevitably leave us shocked by the difficult adjustments that confront many large index constituents. As former beneficiaries of Asia's asset and price inflation, the past's winners are today's losers. The list of today's losers is long: real estate companies in Hong Kong; conglomerates around Asia; heavily indebted companies; and politically connected companies. However, the winners are not immediately obvious. The historical results of companies do not provide guidance on the future impact of Asia's deflation, making thoughtful analysis ever more important and challenging.

...WHILE OTHERS MAY BECOME THE NEW WINNERS

As an example, last week we visited Café de Coral, the leading fast-food operator in Hong Kong, managed by the honest and capable Lo family. Café de Coral was an undeserved loser from Hong Kong's asset and price inflation of the prior decade. Not surprisingly, the stock is right where it was eight years ago despite higher sales and profits. However, our visit revealed the potential for substantial cost savings over the next few years from Hong Kong's deflation in Café de Coral's three major costs: food, labor and real estate. What is less clear, yet equally important, is how sales will perform in Hong Kong's deflationary environment. Will the cost savings be offset partially or totally by lower meal prices? Uncovering the new winners takes lots of thought.

The bear market had upended the corporate landscape. Where would the chips fall? There would be opportunity for some companies to move ahead, and in those companies there would be opportunity for Overlook. As we mention in the next section, our enthusiasm was building.

THE INFLECTION POINT

I wrote a piece at Marc Faber's request for *The Gloom, Boom & Doom Report* in October 1998, the month that proved to be the bottom of the market; the inflection point of long-awaited recovery. No one could be certain that we were truly out of the woods yet; but reform was being addressed by governments and by companies, and we as investors were starting to perceive a path ahead. An excerpt from that piece follows:

When Marc asked me to consider writing a piece for *The Gloom, Boom & Doom Report* on small companies in Asia, two thoughts entered my mind.

My immediate reaction was, why in the world should I consider exposing my leprosy to the public by admitting that I invest in small companies in Asia for a living? Better that I suffer ignominy in private, isolated from the investment community. After all, I have a family to protect, if not a reputation. My loyal, yet depressed, group of investors have heard enough of my exhortations about the valuations and quality of certain select managers. Why try and sell this snake oil to innocent bystanders?

My second thought was that I realized it is every fund manager's nightmare to have Marc Faber, who is known as "Doctor Doom" in Asia, become interested in your asset class. Basically, it means that you and your stocks have been diced, quartered, and shredded, and wheeled to the isolation ward. How could my asset class have performed so miserably? Asian stocks that fell 90% have now fallen another 90%. The dash for the exit has been largely indiscriminate and quite a sight to see, let alone experience. To be fair and objective, Asian leaders and management have poured enough gasoline on themselves to ensure that the stampede was unavoidable, well deserved, and downright satisfying to watch, especially in markets or stocks where my exposure was limited.

So, here I sit in Hong Kong, in late October 1998, and you know what? My enthusiasm is building. For the first time in 18 months, I am not everyone's biggest problem. Asian governments are reforming and our entrepreneurs are back at the factories. The three- to five-year outlook is looking more mouthwatering by the day. Less competition, lower input costs, better investment opportunities, better profit margins, less debt financing, tighter business focus. In short, higher returns on equity.

December 1998: New Winners

▼ OVERLOOK PERFORMANCE:
DOWN 56.4% FROM PEAK

THE BEAR MARKET IS OVER!

Stock Market Performance – Q4 1998

• Hong Kong Up 27.5%

• Korea Up 81.3%

• Thailand Up 40.2%

• Indonesia Up 44.1%

AT LONG LAST...

Though Overlook remained down 56.4% from the peak of May 1997, the portfolio had achieved gains in each of the final four months of the year. Markets across the region were on the rebound, and with a sigh of relief, we at long last could look ahead to more constructive conditions in 1999.

From our December 1998 report:

> We at Overlook are looking forward to 1999. We feel investors will tire of recapping banks and conglomerates; they will search for well-managed, strongly capitalized, efficient companies. As this demand for value and quality unfolds, small buying volume will push the portfolio ahead, as we have seen in Thailand and Korea. Across Asia, business conditions for our companies remain challenging. Consumer spending, industrial production, selling prices and exports are still falling. While we see signs of improvement and reasons for future optimism, there is no denying that it is difficult for most businesses to grow profits.

OUTLOOK FOR 1999–2001

Looking ahead over the next few years, I would like to discuss a few subjects that are important to the outlook for investors in Asia.

First, Asia is, and should remain for the foreseeable future, cash flow positive at almost every level. The countries are running current account surpluses, the companies are cash flow positive and paying down debt, and individuals have slashed discretionary spending and increased savings. For investors in the region, this must be a positive long-term indicator of Asia's inherent competitiveness, and a sign that successful businesses in Asia have value.

Second, we are convinced the earnings environment will dramatically improve over the coming three years. 1997 and 1998 were years of cutting costs, paying off debts, getting out of non-core businesses and getting out of joint ventures in China. Capex is now near zero in Asia. In essence, 1997 and 1998 were years of lowering corporate break-even points. The pick-up in the economies of Asia will handsomely reward those select companies that had either the fewest problems or the best businesses. We look forward to the days when it will not require a Herculean effort to show growing profits.

Third, we feel the importance of corporate reform has become broadly accepted over the past nine months, incorporating more Western business philosophies than ever before. While reform is critical to the very survival of many companies, we expect that improved business practices in Asia will generate benefits for all listed companies. Corporate reform will include greater corporate disclosure, heightened focus on core businesses, and increased attention to lowering cost of capital. We welcome this development, albeit overdue.

Our investment strategy remains firmly focused on securing winners in an environment of deflation, deregulation, and minimal pricing power. We search for companies with flexible cost structures, exporters with clear low-cost advantage, companies with leading domestic franchises, companies that bring innovation to their products and services, companies with net cash, and companies that have a proven ability to self-finance their growth. We see no reason to alter our approach at this time.

ASIA'S NEW WINNERS

From the wreckage of 97/98, a new generation of Asian companies emerged which had learned how to create long-term value. Debt was aggressively repaid and capex was minimized. Earnings, cash flow, returns on equity, and dividends rose. These were Asia's New Winners: companies that Overlook had long worked to identify, and which we now sought to own at the bargain valuations identified in our December 1998 report.

We found just enough of the New Winners to stay relevant and remain in business. Notable executives and companies from the aftermath of 97/98 included the following, many of whom we feature at various points throughout this book:

- Michael Chan, Chairman, Café de Coral (see "The Overlook Investment Philosophy").

- Paul Cheung and Patrick Chan, Co-Founders, Kingboard Chemical (see "Chasing Rainbows: China 1985–2000").

- Surachai Sirivallop, President & Director, Thai Reinsurance (see "Voracious! The 1997/98 Asian Crisis").

- Neil Montefiore, CEO, MobileOne.

- Pramukti Surjaudaja, President, Bank NISP.

- Tan Sri Dato' Lee Shin-cheng, Executive Chairman and CEO, IOI (see "We Don't Invest in China Because China… Is China: 2000–2013").

- Thiraphong Chansiri, President, Thai Union Frozen Food (see "Lessons from Bear Markets").

In many ways, the survival and emergence of these New Winners from 97/98 was also the survival and emergence of Overlook. We got through the crisis together—with incredible determination, deaf ears to criticism and at least a bit of gallows humor. All the executives of the companies mentioned above are in our Hall of Fame and many are in the Decade Club of investments we have held for ten years or more. Everyone connected to the Overlook community owes them a debt of gratitude.

Our reward for surviving the 1997/98 Bear Market was an eight-year run of success during which the Overlook portfolio generated average annual compound returns of 20.0% and comfortably surpassed all Asian indices.

The painful challenges inflicted by the 1997/98 Asian Crisis also taught Overlook lasting lessons that are etched into our psyches and permanently incorporated in The Overlook Model. We survived one of the worst bear markets in modern times, and while nothing can replace the actual experience of living through a 97/98, we can share with you some of the lessons we learned in the next chapter.

You need to be standing at the end of a bear market.

— RICHARD H. LAWRENCE, Sr.

Lessons from
Bear Markets

I knew I was going to take the wrong train, so I left early.

— YOGI BERRA

ALL BEAR MARKETS, let alone those on the scale of 1997/98 or 2007/08, teach investors tough love. Bear markets are a 15-round prize fight with "Smokin' Joe" Frazier, one of the most smothering heavyweight boxers of all time. Smokin' Joe left you banged up and so does a bear market. Investors endure never-ending rounds of pummeling, confusion, dizziness, getting knocked down and struggling to get up, interspersed with short periods of insecure enthusiasm when one of your stocks just stops free falling. Bear markets test you, not just professionally, but emotionally as well.

Bear markets are also opportunities for learning. With that in mind, in this chapter we share the lessons that we at Overlook have learned from bear markets.

Survive

The first and most important lesson of all bear markets is that you must survive. Like losing your last dollar at the blackjack table, or not making it to the finish line, well, if you don't survive, you are out.

Bear Markets Hurt

My favorite analogy to describe bear markets is that they act as a flushing of a toilet. The weak get flushed and the strong survive. Bear markets are the ultimate test of survival of the fittest—especially big Bear Markets like the 1997/98 Asian Crisis, the 2007/08 Global Financial Crisis, and China's 2007/13 Bear Market. Bear markets second guess all assumptions, probe all corporations for weaknesses and vulnerabilities, and treat everyone as guilty until proven innocent. Inevitably, many individuals, companies, and even countries get flushed. And that is always a good thing for long-term investors.

In 26 major bear markets from 1929 to today, the average stock market decline was 38.1%. The worst decline was during the Great Depression, which destroyed 89.2% of investors' money. The 11 bear markets in Asia since 1990 have brought average declines of 38.3%.

Bear markets particularly hurt two categories of stocks: first, companies that are heavily indebted and financially overextended; and second, the stocks that are the hottest momentum plays in the last stage of bull markets. These two categories easily explain the pullback that exceeded 72.3% in 2007/08 in Chinese A-Shares and confirm the danger of comfortable trades, when investors are complacent about risk and valuation.

The following table presents data on the decline of major indices during major bear markets in Asia and the U.S.

Decline of Major Bear Markets

Beginning	Ending	Highest	Lowest	Index	% Decline
Sep-29	Jul-32	381.2	41.2	DJIA	-89.2%
Mar-37	Mar-38	194.4	99.0	DJIA	-49.1%
Sep-39	Apr-42	155.9	92.9	DJIA	-40.4%
May-46	Oct-46	212.5	163.1	DJIA	-23.2%
Dec-61	Jun-62	734.9	535.8	DJIA	-27.1%
Feb-66	Oct-66	995.2	744.3	DJIA	-25.2%
Dec-68	May-70	985.2	631.2	DJIA	-35.9%
Jan-73	Dec-74	1,051.7	577.6	DJIA	-45.1%
Sep-76	Mar-78	1,014.8	742.1	DJIA	-26.9%
Apr-81	Aug-82	1,024.1	776.9	DJIA	-24.1%
Aug-87	Oct-87	2,722.4	1,738.7	DJIA	-36.1%
Jul-90	Sep-90	192.8	136.5	Asia ex-Japan	-29.2%
Jul-90	Oct-90	2,999.8	2,365.1	DJIA	-21.2%
Jan-94	Jan-95	449.0	304.2	Asia ex-Japan	-32.2%
Jul-97	Sep-98	406.5	136.8	Asia ex-Japan	-66.3%
Feb-00	Sep-01	349.3	149.1	Asia ex-Japan	-57.3%
May-01	Oct-02	11,337.9	7,286.3	DJIA	-35.7%
Apr-02	Apr-03	231.2	161.7	Asia ex-Japan	-30.1%
Apr-04	May-04	284.4	223.8	Asia ex-Japan	-21.3%
Oct-07	Oct-08	686.9	230.9	Asia ex-Japan	-66.4%
Oct-07	Mar-09	14,164.5	6,547.1	DJIA	-53.8%
Apr-11	Oct-11	596.1	416.1	Asia ex-Japan	-30.2%
Apr-15	Jan-16	642.6	435.4	Asia ex-Japan	-32.2%
Jan-18	Oct-18	776.2	571.4	Asia ex-Japan	-26.4%
Jan-20	Mar-20	713.7	500.8	Asia ex-Japan	-29.8%
Feb-20	Mar-20	29,551.4	18,591.9	DJIA	-37.1%

Average Decline	-38.1%
Average Asia ex-Japan Decline	-38.3%
Average U.S. Decline	-38.0%
Average except 1929	-36.1%

Note: Data combine overlapping bear markets.

Prepare for Bear Markets,
Don't Predict

At Overlook we say we can't predict the next bear market, but we can prepare for it today and tomorrow. In particular, balance sheets take on greater importance in the opening acts of bear markets, a time that our friend David Scott aptly calls the "time of discovery." As Warren Buffett famously said, "It's only when the tide goes out that you learn who's been swimming naked." Getting balance sheets wrong in a bear market multiplies the pain. Overlook believes balance sheets matter all the time, not just once bear markets start.

Appreciate the
Cap on Subscriptions

A certain percentage of investors will always get caught in a liquidity squeeze, or panic at the unfolding of a bear market, and redeem. This may not be your fault, but it is your problem as a fund manager. It is essential to replace the redeeming capital with new investors so that the fund is not forced to sell the crown jewels. A legal Cap on Subscriptions (see chapter on Business Practices for a full explanation), if managed properly, can provide a backlog of investors interested to invest as others run for cover. This aspect of the Cap worked perfectly for Overlook in the 1997/98 and 2007/08 Bear Markets, when our largest investor redeemed both times.

Never Question the Investment Philosophy

The Overlook Investment Philosophy is our Roadmap. If the fund is down 30% in a bear market, the Roadmap is not the reason why. At times of great uncertainty, don't blame the Roadmap or pull out another map, no matter how shiny and tempting it looks.

Our experience over three decades has shown that the Overlook Investment Philosophy works well in both good times and bad, and in times of inflation and deflation. The validity of our fundamental approach has been tested in past bear markets and gives us great confidence for the next bear market that will inevitably occur. Strong dedication to fundamental research by the Investment Team at Overlook is embedded in the core of our culture and our Investment Philosophy. This commitment to execution is extremely valuable and we see no major need to alter the way we undertake our investment analysis.

Four-Part Strategy to Survive Bear Markets

The following excerpt from our December 2008 quarterly report describes Overlook's response to the 07/08 Bear Market. No two bear markets are alike, but with hindsight this checklist, which we wrote near the end of the Bear Market, is not too bad.

1. INVEST IN NET CASH AND CASH FLOW POSITIVE COMPANIES

In any bear market, it is critical to become cash flow positive and maintain a net cash position. This is as true for companies, including those in Asia, as it is for individuals, institutions, countries, and Wall Street banks. Until companies achieve this position, they remain at risk of floundering, being distracted by problems, losing market share, or ultimately, going bankrupt.

The sooner companies get cash flow positive and show net cash balance sheets, the faster they can take advantage of the bear market to strengthen their businesses and improve profitability. We witnessed this in 1997/98 and we have seen it again in 2008.

2. CONCENTRATE ON COMPANIES WITH PRICING POWER

Over the past 17 months, Overlook has placed great importance on owning companies with pricing power due to our concern over rising global inflation. In 2007, Overlook created a formula that helped us to identify companies with strong pricing power. The equation is based on our belief that companies with a high level of pricing power have shown an ability to earn high cash gross profit margins with low volatility through economic cycles.

Overlook has utilized the insights from this formula to identify companies that we no longer care to own, as well as companies that we really want to maintain or add to the portfolio. After the turmoil of the past few months, and having witnessed how inflation turned into disinflation almost overnight, we can confirm that the benefits of pricing power are equally valuable during periods of falling prices. In fact, I believe that in two years' time everyone will look back to 2008 and wish they had added even more companies with pricing power to their portfolios.

The result of Overlook's focus on pricing power in the last year and a half is that five of our top 17 positions have more than 50% market share, and 16 of 17 hold leading market share in their respective sectors. While we did not set out to construct a portfolio comprised of dominant market share companies, it makes sense that such companies generally have pricing power. Overlook's search for companies with pricing power has been one of the few bright spots of 2008 and should help us for years to come.

3. PREVENT OVERLOOK FROM BECOMING A VALUE TRAP

Over the past months I have become acutely aware that funds, whether they are hedge funds, mutual funds, or investment partnerships, can become value traps under certain conditions that make them uninvestable for individuals and institutions. Let me explain.

In recent years many funds have grown assets under management too quickly, mostly on the back of heavily promoted short-term performance. As the funds accumulated assets, a larger percentage of net assets was allocated into high-risk asset classes in search of alpha and coveted performance. With the onset of the bear market and a surge in redemptions by investors, many funds are now finding themselves trapped between a need to sell their liquid positions to meet redemptions and a desire to limit illiquid positions so as to ensure these do not become an ever-increasing percentage of a fund's net assets. Failure to navigate through this trap has led numerous investment managers to gate their funds or create side pockets under the guise of protecting investors. In my view, this is an admission that they mismanaged their portfolios, as well as a reflection of their excessive greed in the asset accumulation game.

As always, Overlook has the Cap on Subscriptions to thank for avoiding the traps.

4. COMMIT TO DISCIPLINES OF "OLD-FASHIONED" INVESTING

I believe that as the world emerges from this synchronized bear market and recession, investors will yearn to see a return to traditional investment values and asset classes. In such a world, cash flow, high rates of return on equity, dividends, honest management, reasonable valuations, and fair investment structures will prevail—everything Overlook holds dear and has always sought for its investors. In this old-fashioned world, there will be no need to change or reinvent the Overlook Business Model. As a result, I think there will be a great deal of potential interest in our holdings.

Solutions are Found at Factories and Headquarters, Not the Bloomberg Machine

A common failing of investment managers during bear markets is that they focus too much of their time on trying to predict the macroeconomic future. They cease to execute fundamental research at the company level. This inevitably leaves the manager staring at a Bloomberg terminal, paralyzed by the falling share prices and afraid of the telephone. Investment managers compound their difficulties by owning portfolios with too many names and by creating funds filled with too many investors who were chasing unrealistic short-term returns in the "good old days."

At Overlook, our tasks are repetitively clear: visit a well-selected list of companies, undertake intensive analysis of businesses that meet disciplined investment requirements, focus the portfolio on cash flow positive businesses, and engage in a positive manner with the managements of our companies.

Investment Opportunities Improve During Bear Markets

Valuations near the end of bear markets become so compelling that years later you wonder how stocks ever got that cheap. This is the reward for all the pain. In 97/98 and 07/08, valuations fell and then fell and then fell some more just to kick us while we were down.

Most investors have few nice things to say about bear markets, and in most respects, I agree with them. However, bear markets do have a wonderful side to them. They act as a self-correcting mechanism and force changes on economies, companies, consumers and investors that form the basis for valuable and durable recoveries. As the weak get flushed, IPO markets close, assets are marked down, and change begins in earnest. Capital becomes scarce and owners of capital naturally earn higher returns. Irrational competition ends and favorable industry conditions are left for the survivors. Raw materials and input costs drop and make profit margins wider and expansion projects more profitable. Macroeconomic and bank loan growth remain slow, but improved market share and self-financed growth drive earnings higher.

The more severe the bear market, the more dramatic and beneficial the changes. Hard to believe, but history shows this to be true. During the first five years after the 97/98 and 07/08 Bear Markets, Overlook compounded at a rate of 17.9% and 32.2%, respectively, comfortably outpacing the benchmark both times.

Here are the valuations of the portfolio in early 1999, three months off the bottom, at 4.8 times current E.P.S. estimates; and the valuation of the portfolio in early 2009, three months off the bottom, at 7.6 times current E.P.S. estimates. In retrospect, both are hard to believe.

The Earnings Digest

1997/98		2007/08	
Valuation		*Valuation*	
P/E Ratio		P/E Ratio	
1998	5.2×	2007	10.9×
1999E	4.8×	2008E	9.1×
2000E	3.5×	2009E	7.6×
1999E EV/ EBITDA	2.8×	2008E EV/ EBITDA	6.4×
1999E Yield	5.2%	2008E Yield	5.8%
Price to Book Value	0.71×	Price to Book Value	1.62×
Growth and Profitability		*Growth and Profitability*	
1999E Return on Equity	17.0%	2008E Return on Equity	23.7%
Financial Strength & Size		*Financial Strength & Size*	
Net Cash to Equity 1999E	0.11:1	Net Cash to Equity 2008E	0.20:1
Capital Adequacy Ratio 1999E	31.5%	Capital Adequacy Ratio 2008E	17.4%
Sales	US$ 392.6 mm	Sales	US$ 1,466 mm
Profits	US$ 50.6 mm	Profits	US$ 166 mm
Median Market Capitalization	US$ 310.3 mm	Median Market Capitalization	US$ 885 mm

"The Old Winners Are the New Losers, and the Old Losers Are the New Winners."

James Squire, Overlook's Chief Investment Officer, and I often compare notes from our experiences during 1997/98. Though James was not yet at Overlook, having joined us in 2007, we both learned from the Asian Crisis many of the same lessons, often by having owned the same companies or having lived through the same market gyrations. James and I saw first-hand that the Bear Market of 1997/98, painful as it was, brought sweeping change to the leadership of the Asian business world. Asian corporations survived by abandoning their sloppy habits and adopting the hard-nosed skills of blocking and tackling. We call these the New Winners.

An Enlightened Pioneer

I have never been a fan of aggressive bull markets. They reward undisciplined businessmen, substandard businesses, aggressive investors, and greedy investment bankers. Bull markets introduce aggressive new capital into established industries, often causing a general decline in profit margins and returns on investment. And they inevitably end with a bust, pulling down perfectly good companies in their wake.

The 1997/98 Asian Crisis was the pivotal turning point for corporate performance in Asia. The Real McCoys began to emerge to become the new leaders of the corporate world in Asia. One company that particularly stands out in my mind is Thai Union Frozen Food (TUF), which processed, packaged and sold tuna to the major food companies around the world.

TUF was run by Khun Thirapong, son of the founder. His youth and inexperience initially made me nervous, but he quickly proved to be an exceptionally capable executive. Khun Thirapong was fortunate that TUF was a dollar-based business, which was like gold when local currencies collapsed during the Asian Crisis. But Thirapong did not earn his way into the Overlook Hall of Fame because he ran an export business at the time of currency weakness. He earned his place because TUF was the first domestic company in the Overlook portfolio to commit to high-dividend payout. Many executives have since come to understand the importance of dividends, but in my view Khun Thirapong will go down in history as one of Asia's first enlightened dividend pioneers.

Bear Markets End

There have been 14 distinct bear markets since I joined the equity business in 1981. When I find myself in the midst of one, the most important thing to remember is that bear markets end. They do not go on forever, despite what pundits tell us during times of gut-wrenching declines when our stomachs churn at the latest prices. If you are standing at the end and managed to successfully navigate the bear market, you can win—and win big. Bear markets are among the few periods of time in the investment business when fund managers can deliver investors four to five years of outperformance.

In 26 major bear markets from 1929 to today, the average stock market decline lasted 12.1 months. The longest decline was during the Great Depression, which lasted 35 months. The 11 bear markets in Asia since 1990 lasted an average of 9.1 months.

The duration of my 14 bear markets has ranged from 20 months (Tech Bubble in 2000–01) to one day (October 1987, when Hong Kong declined 41% in two trading days). The average duration, excluding 1987, has been 10.1 months. When I calculate the average of 26 bear markets in the U.S. and Asia going back to 1929, the average duration is 14.5 months. These data on bear market duration are summarized in the following table.

In September 2008 we wrote the following, just one month before the bottom.

> In the 1997/98 Asian Crisis, essentially the entire banking systems in Korea, Thailand and Indonesia went bust. Yet, that Bear Market ended in just 14.7 months. At times during the dark days of 1998 I thought stocks would never stop going down, but they did. And we should not lose sight of that. So far, based on the Asia ex-Japan index, this Bear Market in Asia has been just short of 12 full months. However, the bubble in China distorts the length of the 07/08 downturn in Asia. Partners will recall that investors' love affair with China and the Hong Kong "through train" carried the Asian index to its peak in late October. However, Overlook and

other Asian funds that had measured exposure to China peaked in late July 2007 in line with the U.S. Thus, I believe the duration of the current bear market in Asia has already exceeded 14 months. Accordingly, I believe investors need to consider playing more offense than defense and begin to consider allocations post the current bear market.

Duration of Major Bear Markets

Beginning	Ending	Highest	Lowest	Index	Duration
Sep-29	Jul-32	381.2	41.2	DJIA	35 months
Mar-37	Mar-38	194.4	99.0	DJIA	13 months
Sep-39	Apr-42	155.9	92.9	DJIA	32 months
May-46	Oct-46	212.5	163.1	DJIA	4 months
Dec-61	Jun-62	734.9	535.8	DJIA	7 months
Feb-66	Oct-66	995.2	744.3	DJIA	8 months
Dec-68	May-70	985.2	631.2	DJIA	18 months
Jan-73	Dec-74	1,051.7	577.6	DJIA	23 months
Sep-76	Mar-78	1,014.8	742.1	DJIA	18 months
Apr-81	Aug-82	1,024.1	776.9	DJIA	16 months
Aug-87	Oct-87	2,722.4	1,738.7	DJIA	2 months
Jul-90	Sep-90	192.8	136.5	Asia ex-Japan	2 months
Jul-90	Oct-90	2,999.8	2,365.1	DJIA	3 months
Jan-94	Jan-95	449.0	304.2	Asia ex-Japan	13 months
Jul-97	Sep-98	406.5	136.8	Asia ex-Japan	14 months
Feb-00	Sep-01	349.3	149.1	Asia ex-Japan	20 months
May-01	Oct-02	11,337.9	7,286.3	DJIA	17 months
Apr-02	Apr-03	231.2	161.7	Asia ex-Japan	12 months
Apr-04	May-04	284.4	223.8	Asia ex-Japan	1 months
Oct-07	Oct-08	686.9	230.9	Asia ex-Japan	12 months
Oct-07	Mar-09	14,164.5	6,547.1	DJIA	17 months
Apr-11	Oct-11	596.1	416.1	Asia ex-Japan	6 months
Apr-15	Jan-16	642.6	435.4	Asia ex-Japan	9 months
Jan-18	Oct-18	776.2	571.4	Asia ex-Japan	9 months

Jan-20	Mar-20	713.7	500.8	Asia ex-Japan	2 months
Feb-20	Mar-20	29,551.4	18,591.9	DJIA	1 month

Average Duration	12.1 months
Average Asia ex-Japan Duration	9.1 months
Average U.S. Duration	14.3 months
Average Duration except 1929	9.2 months

Note: Data combine overlapping bear markets.

Quotes on Bear Markets from Overlook and Friends

Before I share some quotes on bear markets, I would like to share a quote about the end of bull markets.

Bear markets eventually recover, and bull markets eventually die. The cyclicality is built-in. During bear markets it sometimes feels that the whole world is crashing down, while bull markets sometimes feel like a complacent paradise.

And it was in one corner of paradise, at a beach resort in the Philippines, that I was enjoying the company of my good friend and fellow fund manager, Eric Sandlund. Our families had traveled together for the holidays at the end of 1993.

Asian markets for the prior two years had experienced a heady bull market. In 24 months, indices in Hong Kong had risen 177%; in Thailand, 136%; and in Jakarta, 138%. Overlook had recorded gains of 191% during that period, and Eric's firm certainly would have enjoyed even better results. On New Year's Eve, Eric and I were seated on the veranda, enjoying a beer and the tropical sunset.

"We've had a couple of great years, Eric," I said.

"True, Richard," he said, "but, we won't see another bull market until we have forgotten about this one."

Eric made that statement at what turned out to be the sunset of the bull market. It would not be until the early 2000s, after the devastation of the 1997/98 Asian Crisis, that Asia would again experience a lasting bull market, at which time we had certainly forgotten the 1992/93 Bull Market.

The one reality that you can never change is that a higher-priced asset will produce a lower return than a lower-priced asset. You can't have your cake and eat it. You can enjoy it now, or you can enjoy it steadily in the distant future, but not both—and the price we pay for having this market go higher and higher is a lower 10-year return from the peak.

— JEREMY GRANTHAM

Bull markets are born on pessimism, grow on skepticism, mature on optimism, and die on euphoria. The time of maximum pessimism is the best time to buy, and the time of maximum optimism is the best time to sell.

— SIR JOHN TEMPLETON

Bear markets are the defining moments for managers.

— RICHARD H. LAWRENCE, Jr.

When they raid the whorehouse, they take the piano player too.

— OLD WALL STREET SAYING

Bear markets are times of discovery.

— DAVID SCOTT, Cha-Am Advisors

You make most of your money in a bear market, you just don't realize it at the time.

— SHELBY CULLOM DAVIS

It is only in a bear market that the value investing discipline becomes especially important because value investing, virtually alone among strategies, gives you exposure to the upside with limited downside risk.

— SETH KLARMAN

New Winners will always keep coming from bear markets due to the creativity of Asia's entrepreneurs.

— RICHARD H. LAWRENCE, Jr.

Calm yourself down and get into System 2 thinking. Like my mother always said, patience is a virtue.

— TED SEIDES

PART TWO

The Overlook Model

In order to do something, you must be something.

— ADMIRAL JAMES STOCKDALE,
the longest-serving and highest-ranking American
POW during the Vietnam War

THE MOST SUCCESSFUL fund management companies, in our experience, operate with a quiet modesty. They worked hard for their success, fought to overcome many challenges, learned from mistakes, and gave credit to others who helped along the way. In a similar way, we credit Overlook's success to our teamwork, to our investors who have provided us long-term capital, to company executives who created incredible value for shareholders, and to The Overlook Model.

The following five chapters document the creation of The Overlook Model in 1991 and its execution by the Overlook team in the decades since. We will first describe the Overlook Investment Philosophy, by which we select companies and structure our portfolio for sustained performance, supported by case studies of companies in which we have invested.

We will then explain how an Investment Philosophy, no matter how effective, does not ensure the delivery of results to investors. The delivery mechanism is driven by business practices, and we will describe how we have intentionally designed the Overlook Business Practices to deliver the results of the Investment Philosophy to our investors.

When these two components work in unity, we show how Overlook generates outperformance over the investment universe, and then nearly guarantees the delivery of that outperformance to investors. The result is what we call the Overlook Margin of Safety, otherwise referred to as the Margin of Safety for Investors.

We are struck by the parallel between Overlook's success and the achievements of companies in our portfolio. For companies to achieve success, they must have a model to create a Superior Business, and then they must also deliver results to shareholders with effective Business Practices in corporate governance and capital management. The combination creates the Margin of Safety for Companies.

The Overlook
Investment
Philosophy

Experience is that marvelous thing that enables you to
recognize a mistake when you make it again.

— FRANKLIN P. JONES,
Humorist and Reporter for the *Saturday Evening Post*

A T OVERLOOK WE are fundamental investors. We seek to identify companies with superior businesses, capable management, and long-term investment prospects. We do not invest in trendy stocks or chase speculative markets. We invest in value. However, identifying value requires method and discipline. The Overlook Investment Philosophy provides us with proven methodologies, built over time, that help us to identify value.

In this chapter we will share with you the principles of our Investment Philosophy, then show those principles at work in the real world with examples of companies in which Overlook has invested.

How did the Overlook Investment Philosophy come to be?

In Failure Are the Seeds of Success

No investor can be successful without experiencing failure. Early successes only lure new investors into complacency about the risks and pitfalls that exist. Failure, however, teaches lessons. I have been helped by mentors and professors, books, the CFA program, and colleagues, but at the end of the day, it was also necessary for me to experience the sensation of driving off the cliff in my Volkswagen.

Allow me to share just a few of the many failed attempts to achieve success that I have made during my investing career.

TIMING IS EVERYTHING

Jonathan Bush, founder of J. Bush & Co., where I worked in the early 1980s, taught me fundamental analysis, the importance of return on equity, how to write a research report correctly, techniques for interviewing company management, the Colombo Question and the Five Point Selling system. He taught me that executing the fundamentals is the path to the objective. Despite Jon's valuable training sessions on Monday mornings and his best intentions to steer a few good stocks my way, my future as a stock picker had some questionable moments.

In 1984, the year Apple introduced the Macintosh, I made a buy recommendation at the unadjusted price of US$ 23.0, expecting near-term price escalation through US$ 32.0 and beyond.

In December 1997, after 13 years of flat performance, Apple finally touched US$ 23.0 for the last time. Of course, if you had followed my advice and held until today, your compound annual return would be, as I had anticipated, 21.6% per year for 37 years…

SUNKEN TREASURE

Chung Wah Shipbuilding was a small shipbuilder located in Kowloon, across the harbor from Hong Kong Island. It was a small cap stock that we owned when I worked at FP Special Assets in the late 1980s. The core business was going nowhere, but the company owned valuable real estate that we figured the Government of Hong Kong would be forced to purchase for their second tunnel under Victoria Harbour.

As we awaited our payoff, Chung Wah announced a related party asset injection from the majority shareholders priced at two times book value. When I eventually deciphered the details, I realized that the asset injected was cash – just cash: the owners sold us $1.00 of cash for $2.00...

LUNCH HOUR IN SINGAPORE

In 2004, there was a Singaporean company called Citiraya Industries that one of my colleagues researched and thought was a good idea. The company recycled discarded electronics parts to extract the precious metals for resale. The numbers looked good, the technology was not complicated, and the economics of cost vs. value were compelling. It was my colleague's recommendation; but, as CIO, the decision to invest was my responsibility. We bought a stake.

On my next trip to Singapore, I went around one afternoon to meet the CFO and tour the company's facilities. There was almost nobody on the factory floor. When I inquired where the employees might be, the CFO replied, "Oh, of course, it's lunchtime." I checked my watch and thought nothing about the workers' odd lunch hour.

Not long after that, the news broke from Singapore: the owner had done a runner and was on the lam. Evidently it was lunch hour all day every day at that fine company...

Years later, Overlook's friends at GMT Research had the following explanation for why the factory was empty:

> The Taiwanese authorities were alerted when scrapped chips that belonged to Citiraya's U.S. clients surfaced in Taiwan. The items should have been crushed and recycled in Singapore. The computer chips were diverted for sale overseas and precious metal extracted from waste was falsely declared. Citiraya had 1,554 suspect transactions worth about US\$ 161 million in fake sales between 2003 and 2005. With the help of his brother, the CEO stole 62 containers of electronic scrap between 2003 and 2004 and had them shipped to buyers in Hong Kong and Taiwan. Ng Teck Lee fled with US\$ 51 million, made from selling used computer chips which Citiraya should have recycled, while 11 people were convicted and jailed.

Overlook sold our shares at a −49.1% IRR after less than a two-year holding period.

OVERLOOK TAKES SHAPE

By 1991, I had ten years' experience as a financial analyst. After hundreds of company visits, and under the generous advice and mentoring of many capable investors, I believed I had a working understanding of fundamental investing.

I walked across Central Hong Kong to visit Marc Faber, to ask if I might sublet a space in his offices, not as an employee, but to be among like-minded investors. Marc's "library" became my office, surrounded by his collection of economics books and, just outside, a constantly broken Xerox machine and his extensive, if idiosyncratic, collections of Mao buttons and slabs of marble painted with provocative Chinese nudes. My office was only a tiny space with a small desk, almost no standing room, and a rickety aluminium guest chair. It was perfect.

I had a sense of my direction and objectives, but my first task was to define the Investment Philosophy for my new company, Overlook Investments. I had to bring structure to my thoughts and I had to make the Investment Philosophy authentic to my process. Most importantly, I had to ensure that it would work and that it would endure.

The Overlook Investment Philosophy has worked and it has endured, proving its effectiveness throughout three eventful decades in Asia. We share a slide from the first presentation in 1992 to potential investors. This is followed by a discussion of each of the four components of the Investment Philosophy depicted in the slide. The Investment Philosophy today remains unchanged except for a few words.

The Investment Philosophy, from Overlook's first presentation in 1992

Overlook Investments Limited

THE INVESTMENT PHILOSOPHY

- ◆ Superior Businesses
- ◆ Superior Company Managers
- ◆ Valuation Discipline
- ◆ Long-term Investment Horizon

The Overlook Investment Philosophy

Overlook's success has always revolved around our Investment Philosophy, which is rigid and demanding, yet flexible. It stands at the core of our investment work and has four key components:

I. **Superior Businesses:** This core requirement has done more than anything else to push us towards investing in the most profitable businesses in Asia and has made an oversized contribution to Overlook's performance over the past 30 years.

II. **Management with Integrity:** Since all businesses are impacted by management's behavior, Overlook's efforts to analyze executives' talent, track records, personalities, and ambitions is incorporated into our day-to-day work.

III. **Bargain Valuations:** We believe attention to valuation brings discipline to our decision-making. In short, valuations matter. No other way to buy stocks has ever made any sense to Overlook.

IV. **Long-Term Investment Horizon:** Life got much simpler when Overlook realized that the only great investments are long-term investments.

Before we begin a closer review of these key components of the Overlook Investment Philosophy, it is important to note that virtually all of our work is built upon the detailed financial analysis of companies. Successful research reveals a company's strengths and weaknesses, risks and opportunities, the fortitude of management, and much more. There is no substitute. An investment philosophy is a powerful tool only when it is supported with insightful analysis.

We now review each of the four aspects of the Overlook Investment Philosophy in more detail.

I. Superior Businesses

Many investors write about the importance of investing in highly profitable businesses. The cash cow, the franchise business, the business with low reinvestment risk, and the business with consistently high returns on investment are all businesses that enjoy superior economics. However, the line I like best comes from Jon Bush, who used to tell me to "pick stocks that are floating downriver."

Below are four characteristics that Overlook believes are typically associated with superior companies that are floating downriver:

1. *High Profitability:* In virtually every case, superior businesses possess high profitability. In addition to being the hallmark of successful business performance, high profitability leads to the generation of free cash flow that makes dividends and equitable corporate governance easy for executives to deliver to shareholders.

2. *Predictable E.P.S. Growth:* E.P.S. growth is a critical driver for success. Few things more negatively impact performance than an unexpected decline in earnings, so we must find high-quality companies that deliver predictable E.P.S. growth. Overlook's experience has shown that the following attributes are commonly found in companies that are able to maintain steady growth: low cyclicality of business; steady demand for its products or services; ability to increase market share; and a track record of consistent earnings over a long period of time.

3. *Successful Allocation of Free Cash Flow:* One critical determinant of future performance is a corporation's allocation of free cash flow between reinvestment for future growth and the return of capital to shareholders via dividends or share buybacks. Effective reinvestment into future growth can be a complicated challenge for management. To be justified, reinvestment must clearly enhance a company's future business.

4. *Dominant Pricing Power:* Pricing power is the most valuable corporate asset. It is valuable in times of recession and equally valuable in times of growth, in times of deflation and in times of inflation. The more pricing power a company has, the better.

SUPERIOR COMPANIES IN ACTION

For Overlook, the four characteristics described above have helped us identify some of the predominant characteristics of superior businesses. However, we emphasize that a superior business can mean different things at different times to different people depending on one's own preferences, location, experiences, etc. Judgment is the always the final arbiter. But the ratios set out above can help.

To illustrate Overlook's judgment of superior companies, we offer the following examples of two companies, Unisteel and Café de Coral. We invested in both successfully. These are vastly different businesses, but each one possesses the financial and operating characteristics of a superior business.

UNISTEEL: SIMPLY SUPERIOR

Our analysis from 2006:

As a student of international economics at Brown University in the late 1970s, I often found myself debating the Phillips curve, money supply creation, international economic development, and the stock market with my dad, who owned an investment management firm in New York. During one of the many downturns in the market (and probably shortly after one of his holdings had just bombed earnings), Dad rolled out his argument for investing in a company that just makes screws. Of course, his message was that companies operating simple and focused businesses are usually the best investments.

His advice stayed with me and caused me to chuckle when I first met Bernard Toh, CEO of Unisteel Technology Limited, a Singapore-listed company that manufactures high spec fasteners—otherwise known as screws. It represented many of the attributes my dad taught me to admire in companies. Unisteel's specialized screws are utilized in hard disk drives (HDD) and other electronic products, most famously holding Apple's iPod together with fasteners so small that I cannot pick them up in my fingers.

OPERATIONAL STRENGTH

Unisteel has established a successful track record in this unglamorous industry due to its operational excellence.

» First, they have a long track record of securing consistently high profit margins despite the challenge of selling to Tier 1 HDD manufacturers who are notoriously tough on suppliers.

» Second, they have consistently offset pressure from rising raw material prices and falling selling prices through improved productivity, added services, and vertical integration.

» Third, they are penetrating ultra-competitive Tier 1 mobile phone manufacturers in such a way that long-term margins will not be sacrificed.

FINANCIAL SUCCESS

Most manufacturers in Asia have a difficult time self-financing growth and paying cash dividends. High working capital and capex requirements place minority investors at the mercy of managements that need to take advantage of them to secure the required equity capital.

In contrast, Unisteel offers investors a rare combination of fast growth that has been self-financed and payment of high cash dividends. How do they do it?

» First, Unisteel utilizes its operating assets in an efficient and productive manner. The turnover of operating assets has averaged 3.15 times over the past six years, way above regional averages that have often hovered nearer 1–1.5 times.

» Second, Unisteel earns consistently high profit margins, averaging 27.8% between 2000 and 2006, with low volatility due to Unisteel's ability to transform a commodity (stainless steel) into a high value-added product at extremely competitive prices.

» Third, Unisteel maintains balance sheet discipline. Minimal corporate funds are devoted to non-productive assets. Non-operating assets have averaged only 11% of total assets over the past six years, a figure that helps supercharge returns.

» Fourth, Unisteel generates large amounts of free cash flow. Capex has averaged only 30.3% of gross cash flow since 2000. This is especially low when compared to the compound growth of revenue of 35.4% over the past six years.

THE RESULT

These financial and operational strengths combine to offer spectacular returns on investment over the past six years:

» Operating return on average operating net assets has averaged 89%.

» Return on average assets has averaged 23%.

» Return on average equity has averaged 37%.

All this has allowed Bernard to adopt an aggressive policy of paying out substantial dividends each year, averaging 61.6% of net income since 2000, a great number given the rapid growth that has exceeded 30% since its IPO in 2000.

What started out as a very mundane, potentially cyclical, and perhaps uninteresting business has ended up with something rare and extremely valuable, and certainly something that my father would have enjoyed owning during the dull days of the late 1970s.

Bernard Toh is a member of the Hall of Fame and we generated an IRR of 37.6% on our investment in Unisteel over 4.1 years. The duration would have been much longer if the company had not sold out to private equity investors.

CAFÉ DE CORAL: HONG KONG'S BEST FAST-FOOD OPERATOR

In this second example of a superior company, we discuss Café de Coral, a company I have followed closely since its IPO in 1986 and in which Overlook first invested in 1998. It is the leading Chinese fast-food operator in Hong Kong, but it is more than a restaurant: it is a great public company run by executives with integrity.

From our September 2007 report:

> Café de Coral is the leading Chinese fast-food operator in Hong Kong. The Company has an enviable long track record on issues of balance sheet management, profit performance and equitable corporate governance. Michael Chan, the company's chairman, leads an experienced management team that is impressive and forward-thinking.
>
> We are delighted that Overlook owns an interest in this cash-generating machine. Over the past nine years gross cash flow has risen from HK$ 256 million in FY 1998 to an estimated HK$ 620 million for the current fiscal year. As a result, Café de Coral has gone from HK$ 131 million of net debt to HK$ 1,243 million of net cash projected for March 2008. An additional HK$ 1,486 million has been paid out in dividends over that time.
>
> Overlook believes that high operating returns are an excellent indicator of companies that generate strong free cash flow. Ten years ago, Café de Coral was generating a 20% operating return

(defined as operating profits over average operating net assets). In the latest fiscal year, the operating return rose to 68.1%.

I believe the combination of free cash flow, high dividends, an experienced management team, and open-ended growth makes the stock an attractive part of our portfolio. Since the inception of our investment, Café de Coral has generated a 30% IRR.

This story, also from our September 2007 report, reminds us where all that excellence actually comes from:

The quality and attractiveness of the Café de Coral outlets were hammered home to me on my recent trip to Hong Kong when I did a bit of comparison shopping. There is a McDonald's at the end of Duddell Street and I wandered in one day at lunch hour. The unit was in the basement down a narrow, twisted flight of stairs. It had low ceilings and felt rather claustrophobic. On the day of my visit, McDonald's offered 11 selections for lunch, the great majority of which were on the menu 10, if not 20, years ago. Limited seating was down another flight of stairs in the sub-basement.

Later that day, I passed by Café de Coral's newest outlet in Central at the end of a shopping arcade on Queen's Road Central. The new store is one of Café de Coral's fourth-generation designs. The contrast between Café de Coral and McDonald's in terms of ambience, cleanliness, and meal selection was huge. Over 22 lunch selections were available on the day of my visit, many of which vary day by day, enabling customers to order new dishes on a daily basis. CdeC's outlet had a modern look, creative lighting, spacious seating, contemporary furniture, and flat screen TVs on the walls. An Oliver's Super Sandwich, also owned by Café de Coral, was attached to the outlet and offered customers an easy alternative to Chinese fast food. One could not help but appreciate that CdeC was intimately in tune with the desires and culture of Hong Kong people. The feel was much closer to a restaurant serving interesting food than the fast-food outlet suggested by its prices.

Michael Chan is a member of the Hall of Fame. Café de Coral is a member of the Decade Club and Overlook generated an IRR of 23.8% over 14.4 years. Overlook has enjoyed few relationships as much as our dealings with Café de Coral's management.

II. Management with Integrity

Overlook has made it a fundamental part of our day-to-day work to analyze management's capabilities, long-term track record, personality, and ambitions.

We work to know our executives by making regular visits to companies. We observe how executives handle the inevitable ups and downs of their businesses and whether they can survive the next bear market. Do they think for the long term? Do they do what they say? How do they talk to us?

Management with Integrity is not a trait that can be scientifically measured, so James Squire, Overlook's Chief Investment Officer, identified four key traits to guide the Investment Team's assessment of management, which we summarize in the acronym, "COLA":

Capital Allocation

Operational Excellence

Leadership/Strategy

Alignment of Interests with All Shareholders

The objective is to identify executives who have operating practices to create a superior business. They must be willing to share value with minority investors. We must further determine whether management effectively delivers that value to shareholders through appropriate corporate governance and capital management practices.

The following stories of two exceptional executives illustrate management with integrity.

TOP GLOVE: TALK LESS, LISTEN MORE

Top Glove Holdings first came to our attention in 2001 when it was preparing for its IPO. We were not yet ready to invest, but followed the company with interest until 2005, when Overlook met with the company's Chairman and founder, Dr. Lim Wee-chai, in Malaysia. During that conversation we became convinced that this impressive executive was going to build a large and successful company. We invested.

From our June 2006 report:

> Top Glove is the world's largest manufacturer and marketer of latex rubber gloves. Its global market share tops 18%. For the year ending August 2006, Overlook expects revenue and net profits to reach US$ 245 million and US$ 22 million, respectively. The return on equity for 2006 should reach 33.0%.

> I recall a visit to Top Glove's headquarters in 2005, before we had made the decision to invest. During a meeting with company executives, Dr. Lim came in to join the discussion. I expected to leave on completion of the meeting, but instead I was led to a small dining room off the main lobby where eight or nine employees were waiting to eat lunch at a round table with Dr. Lim and myself. While these employees were senior, with direct responsibility, they did not represent the highest-ranking executives within Top Glove as might be expected. I was surprised and instantly impressed by how Dr. Lim did not steer the conversation one way or another or demand the stage as the official voice of Top Glove. In fact, he talked less, listened more, and solicited opinions from his colleagues who candidly addressed competition; costs; corporate governance; the challenge of financing a high-growth company; employee stock options; incentive compensation; and many other subjects.

> This is a highly unusual experience in Asia, where underlings commonly defer to the boss, especially in front of outsiders, and it has lingered with me over the years. All the more so when, at later meetings, Dr. Lim and his colleagues discussed important cost

savings which had been suggested by employees and which were then being implemented throughout the company's 12 factories.

That attitude, that inclusiveness, that willingness to listen and to innovate, has made Top Glove a great company and a great investment for Overlook.

In 2010 Dr. Lim was named to the Overlook Hall of Fame. Top Glove generated an IRR of 39.8% over 6.3 years.

PEOPLE'S FOOD: RESTRAINT, FOCUS AND UNDERSTANDING

In this second example of Management with Integrity, we share our good fortune to have met Mr. Zhou Lian-kui, CEO of People's Food Holding Limited.

From our December 2001 report:

> People's Food (PF) is the largest integrated pork processor in China with sales and profits for 2002 estimated to reach US$ 745 million and US$ 100 million, respectively.
>
> The company is owned and managed by Zhou Lian-kui, 42, a confident yet understated entrepreneur. While he is soft spoken, his accomplishments of growing a company to US$ 100 million in profits in less than eight years illustrate his great focus and a natural talent for business. Mr. Zhou's characteristics of restraint, focus and understanding of per-share values match the skills we feel are required for success in China.
>
> At a recent dinner in Tsingtao, I had the opportunity to discuss with Mr. Zhou the challenges posed by running a large private enterprise in China, particularly with its elevated profile as a public company. He reviewed the opportunities offered by an industry with many weak owners. He discussed his competitive advantages over rivals, many of whom are listed in Shanghai and Shenzhen.

He reviewed the productivity improvements that can be realized by acquisitions. However, what was most revealing to me was Mr. Zhou's measured approach toward considering acquisitions. Rather than blasting ahead and compromising on the issue of employees or price, Mr. Zhou insisted several times that his goal is to double production over three years, not one year. Having seen so many entrepreneurs whose eyes are bigger than their stomachs, Mr. Zhou's approach gives Overlook the confidence to support PF with a significant investment.

POSTSCRIPT

People's Food was one of Overlook's early investments in a purely domestic business in China. Mr. Zhou's effective leadership gave us an understanding of how well-managed companies could navigate the challenges and exploit the huge potential of the China market. These lessons would be invaluable to Overlook in the future.

Mr. Zhou's contribution to Overlook far exceeds the 9.8% IRR earned over 8.6 years through our investment in People's Food.

III. Bargain Valuations

It is easy enough to find great companies with the characteristics discussed above, but those with attractive valuations are much more difficult to tease out. What one pays and what one gets are not always aligned. We must have the fortitude to say no when opportunities are inappropriate and continue to hunt for the next idea. This discipline has been critical to Overlook's outperformance over the past 30 years.

Overlook responds to the valuation challenge by utilizing a number of the tools and disciplines at our disposal.

- We create customized financial models on every company we consider. We write a detailed one-page Investment Thesis highlighting the five major drivers of the business, as taught to me by Jon Bush over 40 years ago.

- We segment the portfolio to make sure we are comparing a new idea to comparable stocks. For instance, we don't compare a domestic leader to an infrastructure company. We measure like to like, apples to apples.

- We rely on The Overlook Tower, a detailed database of stocks which, if the price were right, we might buy. By comparing the companies in the Tower to our portfolio, we continually ensure that we own the best of the best. Dan Rupp, a member of the Investment Team with 15 years at Overlook, has enhanced the utility of the Tower beyond what we had ever expected.

- We look to the Overlook Earnings Digest for all the quantitative and qualitative conclusions on each holding and on the portfolio as a whole. The Earnings Digest shows us what we own and how we can improve the mix. More growth for same profitability? Higher profitability for lower valuation? And so forth. These are questions designed to ensure new ideas are accretive to the existing portfolio.

- How does our portfolio compare today vs. its history? We have three decades of portfolio data to inform us.

- We utilize the Overlook Equation, created 38 years ago and updated recently. This equation is a benchmark, not an absolute, and is used to help de-emotionalize the investment process by giving us a sense of value against profitability and growth. The equation pushes us toward highly profitable businesses, as opposed to rapidly growing businesses. High profitability gives free cash flow, which in turn gives dividends and better corporate governance.

$$\frac{\text{Normalized E.P.S. Growth Rate} + \text{Operating Return}}{\text{P/E Ratio}} = \text{Value Score}$$

IV. Long-Term Investment Horizon

*I often lobby the chairmen and managing directors of our companies
to recognize that the race is a marathon, not a 100-yard dash. Time
passes quickly and sustainable performance is more important, and
harder to achieve, than most executives believe. It is also critical to
the performance of Overlook.*

— RICHARD LAWRENCE, 1996

The compounding effect of earnings over the long term is powerful.
Anticipating a company's future earnings gets much easier with a consistent
track record of performance. For Overlook, a track record is a gold mine
for deep financial analysis. As we got to know Fuyao Glass in late 2013,
we identified many strengths; in particular, its 15-year track record of
consistent growth and profitability.

PAST PREDICTS FUTURE: FUYAO GLASS

From our March 2015 report:

> Fuyao is the largest auto glass company in China with a 63% share
> of the China automotive market. Fuyao is five times larger than its
> nearest rival in China and operates 12 manufacturing plants spread
> across the mainland near production facilities of major OEM vehicle
> manufacturers. Fuyao sells to all major OEM vehicle manufacturers
> in China and overseas and is one of the few Chinese auto parts
> companies that has penetrated the top auto companies not only in
> China but worldwide. International sales equal 35% of revenue, an
> area that Overlook expects will expand in the coming years.

GROWTH AND PROFITABILITY

Following are two 15-year charts. The first one shows various
profit margins; and the second, growth of sales, operating profits,

net profits and dividends in renminbi. Both charts highlight the impressive achievements of Fuyao over the past 15 years and give us confidence about the future.

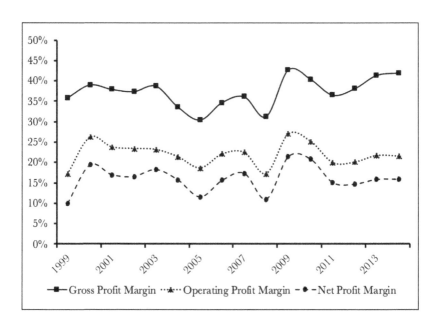

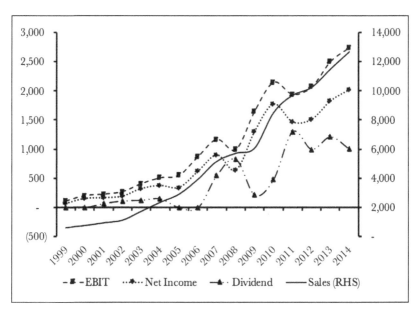

FUYAO'S FINANCIAL MODEL

For the past 15 years, Fuyao has grown revenue and E.P.S. at compound growth rates of 22.4% and 25.3%, respectively. Over the same 15-year period, Fuyao has averaged a 49% dividend payout ratio. In 2003 Fuyao went public in China and raised Rmb 581 million. Since that time, the company has paid out over Rmb 6.8 billion in cash dividends. Fuyao has done admirable work on behalf of shareholders and Overlook believes it can look forward to more of the same in the future.

THE END RESULT

Overlook generated an IRR of 23.3% over 5.8 years from our investment in Fuyao.

The Overlook Pyramid: Generating Outperformance

If you can execute the Investment Philosophy correctly, if you can find those special companies that meet the rigors of the Investment Philosophy, if you can find the next Unisteel or Fuyao, and if you can do it over a long period of time, then the reward for your hard work is within your grasp.

The power of executing the Investment Philosophy is depicted in what we call The Overlook Pyramid.

The Overlook Pyramid

High ROE
Low Debt

Superior
Businesses

**Universe
of Stocks**

Low ROE
High Debt

Mistakes

Think of the Pyramid as the universe of all market cap appropriate public companies in Asia.

At the top of the Pyramid are the small collection of companies that have characteristics we have described in this chapter. These are the select few. Many of these end up in the Overlook Hall of Fame and the Decade Club.

At the bottom of the Pyramid are those run-of-the-mill companies that do not earn high returns and are unable to deliver predictable growth due to failings of their business. Many are managed by executives who are primarily concerned with extracting value for themselves at the expense of minority shareholders. A large percentage run chronically cash flow negative businesses that bounce from one capital raising to another. When Overlook finds itself owning one of these companies, we simply call it a mistake.

Now, let us explain the true power of the Overlook Investment Philosophy. If investors can manage to push their portfolio toward the top of the Pyramid and keep it there for at least a five-year period, then that portfolio is positioned to generate outperformance over the universe.

"Outperformance" is a strong word in the investment world and not something we say lightly.

There are two caveats. First, investors cannot badly overpay for these great companies. Even modest overpayment detracts from outperformance. Foolish overpayment eliminates all the hard work undertaken to identify superior businesses run by great executives. Second, as the size of the fund grows ever larger, a higher proportion of holdings will overlap with the universe and put at risk the fund's ability to generate non-correlated gains.

Overlook has owned just enough companies at the top of the Pyramid to compound net asset value per share at 14.3%. We outperformed the universe by 6.5 percentage points per year for 30 years. More importantly, we delivered 14.2% returns to the Overlook investors. We outperformed when we were a small fund, we outperformed when we were a mid-sized fund, and we continue to outperform as a large fund. We outperformed when I made every stock pick and we have continued to outperform now that I make almost none of the stock picks.

The only logical and believable explanation is that the success was generated by the consistent execution of the Overlook Investment Philosophy.

Delivering Results to Investors

We mentioned earlier in this chapter that outperformance of the portfolio over a universe is created by the investment philosophy, and that value is delivered to Overlook's investors by effective business practices. The investment philosophy and business practices must interact. One without the other is not enough.

This can also be thought of as an equation:

Investment Philosophy + Business Practices = Success for Investors

The same principle holds true for corporations. Overlook searches for superior corporations that can both create value with excellent operating practices and deliver that value to shareholders with effective business practices through excellent corporate governance and capital management. A company's operating practices and business practices must interact.

This can be thought of as an equation:

Superior Business + Business Practices = Success for Corporations

Rarely do things go well for fund managers or businesses when business practices go wrong. In the next chapter, we tell the shocking story of a failed delivery system in the investment management industry.

Failure to Deliver

Once in the dear dead days beyond recall, an out-of-town visitor was being shown the wonders of the New York financial district. When the party arrived at the Battery, one of his guides indicated some handsome ships riding at anchor. He said, "Look, those are the bankers' and brokers' yachts."

"Where are the customers' yachts?" asked the naïve visitor.

— FRED SCHWED, Jr.,
Where Are the Customers' Yachts? (1940)

W E EXPLAINED IN the previous chapter how the Overlook Investment Philosophy has generated outperformance over the universe over the past three decades. We also mentioned that effective business practices are required to deliver that outperformance to Overlook's investors. One without the other is not enough.

We all know the ramifications of a failed investment philosophy. But what happens when business practices fail?

I read the following story in the financial press in 2010. Its reverberations remain as powerful as though I had read it yesterday.

The CGM Focus Fund, managed by Ken Heebner, has been named the "best performing U.S. diversified stock mutual fund of the decade" by Morningstar. According to the *Wall Street Journal*, the CGM Focus Fund produced time-weighted returns (TWR) of 18% over the past 10 years. Yet Morningstar showed that, when measured for capital-weighted returns (CWR), underlying investors actually *lost* 11% on average per year for the same period. That is a discount equal to 29 percentage points every year for a decade. In other words, the average investor actually lost money by investing with the "best-performing" U.S. diversified stock mutual fund!

Stories like this are shocking, yet needlessly common in the world of investment management. Something is wrong when such a dramatic discount can exist between the performance of a fund and the performance that a fund manager delivers to clients.

How is that discount even possible?

First Our Story Needs Some Definitions

- *Time-weighted return (TWR):* This calculates the compound growth of the Net Asset Value of a portfolio, on a per-share basis, over a specified period of time. This is the number you see promoted by fund managers when you open up the newspaper.

- *Capital-weighted return (CWR):* This calculates the Internal Rate of Return (IRR) for both an individual investor's return and the return collectively earned by all investors in the fund. The CWR accounts for all cash flows into and out of the investor's specific account and the fund since inception. This number almost never appears in public for reasons we will explore later.

- *The Discount (the "Discount") and the Premium:* This is the difference between the TWR and the CWR for a specific fund. Discounts occur when CWRs underperform TWRs.

A large discount between TWR and CWR is a sure sign of failed business practices. This is explained in the following report from December 2010.

ONE OF WALL STREET'S DIRTY LITTLE SECRETS

Shortly after Overlook's inception, a rather stern former Swiss client of mine requested that I include capital-weighted return (CWR) figures in our monthly statements. Not knowing better, I naively added this information. I have provided all Overlook investors with individual and partnership CWR information in monthly and quarterly reports ever since. I have always liked the fact that Overlook provides each investor with the results of their specific investment since inception with Overlook. As someone who is married to an early Apple marketing executive, I feel it is a good example of truth in advertising. Investors are happy with Overlook, or they are not. Either way, their own personal performance is absolutely clear and legitimate.

This brings me to 2010, when a certain aspect of Overlook's performance history smacked me in the face, highlighting an incredibly important lesson about performance and investing.

Hedge fund managers and other aggressive asset gatherers might prefer to stop reading now, as my story and my opinions may not be appreciated.

STUDIES ON TIME- AND CAPITAL-WEIGHTED RETURNS AND THE DISCOUNT

The fact that CWR underperforms TWR for most funds is a well-established but unrecognized problem for investors.

I first came across the Discount when I read a research study in the early 1980s about the Magellan Fund and Peter Lynch, one of my heroes. The report showed (and I can't remember the specific numbers or find the actual study) that while Peter Lynch was producing world-leading returns at Magellan, underlying investors actually performed far worse.

David Swensen of the Yale Investment Office has also highlighted the Discount suffered by investors in tech mutual funds during the Internet bubble of 2000 in the entertaining chapter titled "Chasing Performance" in his book, *Unconventional Success*.

Jack Bogle of Vanguard has written extensively about the Discount as well. In his book, *Enough*, Mr. Bogle opined that CWRs trailed TWRs in the indices by an average of 5 percentage points per year over the 25 years leading up to 2005.

WHY THE DISCOUNT?

There are two principal causes of the Discount.

First, a fund manager can generate exceptional results as measured by TWRs at the inception of the fund when assets under management (AUM) are small. Then the manager gets "discovered" and/or "promoted" and an explosion of money enters the fund, to the great delight of the fund manager. However, with the larger asset base, the now-famous fund manager performs poorly, dragging down his TWR while crushing his CWR.

Second, CWRs are hurt when investments are poorly timed. Investors chase funds promoting hot themes, then bail out when markets turn down. This behavior inevitably decreases their CWRs. But even buying smartly and selling poorly, or buying poorly and selling smartly, can result in a Discount.

On average, the Discount increases when some of the following conditions prevail:

» Funds experience fast growth of assets under management: the Discount tends to increase as the absolute value of a fund increases.

» Funds are invested in trendy asset classes.

» Funds are exposed to excessive valuation risk.

» Funds have excessive exposure to fund-of-funds' investors.

» Funds are operated in higher volatility sectors.

WHO IS RESPONSIBLE?

Fund managers inevitably blame investors for both principal causes of the Discount. You can just hear them, can't you? "I didn't write the check." "Fast growth of assets under management won't impact my performance." "I told the investor not to redeem at the bottom of the bear market." "Yes, fund-of-funds' investors comprise 45% of my assets under management, but they have made a long-term commitment." "Yes, the fund has risen a lot, but P/Es are still relatively cheap."

I don't buy these excuses and feel that individual fund managers, and the wider asset management industry, are complicit in the Discount and conveniently guilty of casually brushing off responsibility for CWRs. Fund managers should "own" their CWRs and disclose them.

CAN THE DISCOUNT BE ELIMINATED?

This is where our depressing story gets more interesting.

While much has been written about the Discount, almost nothing that I have found has been written about the near-guaranteed ability of fund managers to eliminate the Discount. Yes, I did say, "near-guaranteed" ability of fund managers to eliminate the Discount.

Overlook, as shown in this updated chart, has eliminated the Discount over just about every time period from year 1 to year 30.

Updated as of May 31, 2021	Capital -Weighted Return	Time -Weighted Return	Outperformance CWR over TWR*
5 years	18.4%	17.1%	1.1%
10 years	13.3%	12.7%	0.5%
20 years	16.7%	17.2%	-0.5%
Since Inception (30 years)	14.2%	14.3%	-0.1%

* Calculated by geometric compounding.

It initially took some time to understand the reasons why Overlook has been able to eliminate the Discount, but after 12 years of operation I finally found the answer. The elimination of Overlook's Discount is overwhelmingly due to our legal Cap on Subscriptions. There is no other plausible explanation.

This achievement is not due, as I first thought, to the success of our Investment Philosophy or the luck of our investors in timing their investments. Our Investment Philosophy has helped us achieve outperformance of our TWR vs. the benchmark, but it has had no impact on CWR. The luck of the investors is not a factor either, as our investors have added funds to Overlook consistently over time. No, the answer lies exclusively in the legal Cap on Subscriptions because the Cap has allowed a limited amount of funds to enter steadily over the past 30 years. And control over the growth of AUM is the key to eliminating the Discount. The legal Cap on Subscriptions is the hero of our story today.

WHY DON'T ALL FUND MANAGERS ELIMINATE THE DISCOUNT?

Here is where I become critical of the fund industry. Hedge fund managers and asset accumulators who didn't stop reading before should really stop reading now.

If the Cap allowed Overlook to eliminate the Discount, could all fund managers eliminate their own Discounts if they adopted a legal cap on subscriptions, so as to limit growth of subscriptions consistently to approximately 8–9% per year? My answer is a resounding "Yes."

If managers could deliver between 4 and 9 percentage points per year of additional performance for their investors by embracing the Cap, why on earth wouldn't they? Their clients would be loyal and their business would have an excellent long-term outlook. Well, as we all probably know, Wall Street and the fund management industry are incentivized around the accumulation of AUM and accumulation of their own wealth, not their clients' wealth or the generation of CWRs.

While individual managers can deny this, we only need to look at how few managers report CWR to their investors. Some of Overlook's clients tell us that Overlook is one of the very few that disclose CWR figures. Many hedge fund managers can't let this data out, as it would expose promotion of their TWR performance as misleading and the conflict of interest between them and their investors as huge, if not nearly fraudulent. If you don't believe us, ask all your managers to email you their CWR numbers over 1, 3, 5, and 10 years. Just be forewarned that replies may be few and far between.

IS THE DISCOUNT DANGEROUS TO OVERLOOK'S INVESTORS?

While the community of managers that operate under a cap on subscriptions can offer no guarantees on TWRs, I have come to realize that funds with large Discounts pose real and material risks to investors. For example, during bear markets, a fund with a high Discount would surely be much more prone to redemptions and expose investors to the cost of side pockets or redemption restrictions. Almost certainly, if we accumulated the data on all the funds that side pocketed or restricted redemptions, we would find that a disproportionately large percentage of the funds have what I call a "CWR problem." Or, in other words, a large Discount.

So, I strongly believe that a large Discount is dangerous to investors' health, and that all investors should monitor this number for all their funds. And if your managers don't supply the following four data points, perhaps you need to consider the rationale of your investment.

1. Time-weighted returns

2. Capital-weighted returns

3. Fund AUM

4. Firm-wide AUM

WHO HAS THE LARGEST DISCOUNTS?

What really makes me mad is that it is very probable that some portion of the largest (read: greedy) hedge fund managers have large Discounts despite positive TWRs. Here I am referring to the fast-growing, high-profile 2 and 20 crowd that built their businesses on excellent TWRs when they were small, then happily took in all the big bucks when expansion of AUM followed. It is specifically this group of "performance-based" managers that works to keep their CWRs a deep dark secret.

I respect your talent, but I don't like anything else about you.

— LIEUTENANT COLUMBO,
played by Peter Falk in the 14-year hit TV series, *Columbo*

It's All About Business Practices

What can fund managers do to rectify their Discount? They can change their business practices. To see how, in the next chapter we will discuss how the Overlook Business Practices are expressly designed with the single purpose to deliver returns to our investors.

The Overlook
Business Practices

At Overlook, we seek to deliver superior investment returns by putting the interests of our investors above all else.

— RICHARD H. LAWRENCE, Jr.

O VERLOOK IS IN this business for one purpose: to deliver results to our investors, in terms of capital-weighted returns over time for each investor and the Overlook Community of investors as a whole. That is our measure of success.

We have emphasized in the two previous chapters that time-weighted returns are generated first by the Investment Philosophy, but that those returns must be delivered to Overlook's investors by effective Business Practices. And the delivery of returns to investors is embedded in our Business Practices.

The Overlook Business Practices

Our Business Practices are comprised of policies, procedures and disciplines that work together to deliver capital-weighted results to the Overlook investors. These include the following:

I. We control assets under management with the legal Cap on Subscriptions and by returning capital to the Overlook investors when deemed necessary.

II. We outlaw policies that lead to greed and conflicts of interest.

III. We work to build the Overlook Community of high-quality investors who share our long-term objectives.

IV. We strive to create a culture that embraces diversity, cooperation and hard work.

V. We have a well-established path for transition of ownership at Overlook to the second and third generations of management.

VI. We naturally embrace the fight against climate change and welcome cultural diversity.

VII. We selectively deploy Overlook's unique Modern Finance Technology to improve corporate governance and capital management.

We will now look at each of these Business Practices in more detail.

I. The Overlook Cap on Subscriptions

As we discussed in "Failure to Deliver," the most effective way to deliver capital-weighted results to the Overlook investors is to control assets under management. And the most effective way to control assets under management is to adopt a legal Cap on Subscriptions.

The Overlook Cap on Subscriptions originated in our earliest days, during a lunch in 1992 at the University Club in New York with Crosby Smith, a representative of the Dillon Family. He asked me why I wouldn't just raise capital to generate fees like other investment managers.

"Because," I said, "I just want to pick stocks and invest in Asia." Crosby looked at me skeptically as if to say he had heard that line before. I then continued: "What would you say if I limited initial subscriptions into the fund at $30 million?"

"You do that, Richard, and the Dillon Family will commit $1 million." Crosby shook my hand and Overlook had its first investor. The Overlook Cap on Subscriptions was born in that spontaneous moment.

The Cap on Subscriptions has proven to be the single most significant business decision in our 30-year history, and has had lasting benefits far greater than Crosby or I could have anticipated at that time, including:

- The Cap has lowered the cyclical volatility of assets under management by limiting the inflow of funds at the top of the market and discouraging investors from redeeming at the bottom.

- The Cap has tended to provide a backlog of investors when opportunity beckons, as at the end of a bear market.

- The Cap has incentivized investors to make a long-term commitment to Overlook, in alignment with our long-term investment horizon. Investors usually have to wait 6–12 months to gain access, so there are not short-term gains for investors trying to time the markets.

There have also been two occasions in recent years when outsized gains on Overlook's investments have driven our assets under management to levels we felt compelled to address.

1. By February 2018, assets under management at Overlook had grown in 21 months from US$ 3.7 billion to almost US$ 6 billion, an increase of 61.0%, with 97% of this increase generated from gains recorded on our investments.

2. By February 2021, assets under management at Overlook had grown in 27 months from slightly over US$ 4 billion to almost US$ 7.5 billion, an increase of 83%, with 87% of this increase generated from gains recorded on our investments.

While such gains are terrific news for Overlook's investors in the short term, we know from industry experience that fast asset growth and large assets under management at fund management companies are rarely in their best interest. We therefore decided on both occasions to return US$ 1 billion to Overlook's investors to better concentrate assets on the very best opportunities.

As we reported to our investors in January 2021:

> We take our fiduciary duty to the Overlook investors too seriously to ignore the challenges that arise from fast growth of assets under management. The Overlook Cap on Subscriptions has slowed our asset growth throughout our history, but even the Cap couldn't slow the last 11 years. The simple fact is that our assets had grown faster than is healthy for Overlook and we refuse to trade our reputation and the capital-weighted returns of the Overlook investors for additional fee income.

Controlling AUM also allows us to most effectively structure our portfolio. Overlook believes that owning 20–22 companies in the portfolio offers us the appropriate level of diversification while providing us an information and insight advantage with our holdings. Once the objective of owning 20–22 names was adopted, Overlook established a practice to buy companies with market capitalizations equal to or larger than the AUM of Overlook. These two practices fit hand in glove.

II. Outlaw Policies that Lead to Greed and Conflicts of Interest

In the early 1990s I attended a luncheon for security analysts at the old Hilton Hotel on Queen's Road Central in Hong Kong. There were about 50 attendees seated at six large round tables. At my table was the Managing Director of Hong Kong's largest asset manager, a widely known and well-respected figure.

A discussion arose at our table on soft dollar brokerage fees, which at the time were under investigation in the Hong Kong investment management community. To my surprise, the Managing Director seated across from me spoke in support of soft dollar commissions and made a defense of the practice. Now, soft dollar brokerage fees, in my view, are just stealing from one's clients. I called him out on it. He shrugged as if to say, "Let's agree to disagree." He and his firm fell in my esteem.

How it might be in investors' best interests for me or Overlook to receive financial benefits from our trading is beyond my comprehension. It is a blatant conflict of interest that must be eliminated. We documented our policies in our December 1994 report:

- Overlook Investments and the employees of Overlook Investments do not accept brokerage rebates. The benefit of low brokerage rates accrues to the investors in Overlook, not the management company. We strongly condemn the practice of brokerage rebates and the conflict of interest that it inevitably causes.

- We have cut our management fees 21 times in 30 years to share success with the Overlook Community.

- Overlook Investments Limited and its employees do not buy shares in Asian public companies for their own account. Employees are encouraged to invest directly through Overlook and are not subject to the Cap on Subscriptions. We have the bulk of our personal net worth invested in Overlook. While we strongly believe in eating our own cooking, we feel it is imperative that we eat the same meal as our investors.

- We have no hidden fee or markups: all of Overlook's investors, from the largest to the smallest, pay the same fee.

Alan Morgan, Overlook's COO and CFO, constantly searches for further improvements to the Overlook Business Practices. This effort builds upon the traditions established by his predecessors, Ms. Yuet-mei Lee and Michael Lonergan.

III. Building the Overlook Community

Attracting investors with short-term capital chasing short-term gains cannot succeed for long periods of time. It's almost a law of physics. Inevitably there will be a time when performance will lag and short-term investors will redeem. We have understood since inception that building trusted relationships with high-quality investors was essential for Overlook to achieve long-term performance. Communication is essential. Accordingly, James, Leonie, Alan and I actively maintain timely reporting practices and regular dialogue to enhance the Overlook Community's understanding of, and trust in, Overlook.

The communication effort is managed by Jeannine Medeiros, Natalie Mak and Esther Adams using the systems and procedures established by Jeannine's predecessor, Ellen Zinke. Jeannine, Natalie and Esther updated the Overlook website by incorporating user-friendly navigation tools and improved design to help investors sort through three decades of material. Ellen dedicated 22 years to Overlook before retiring with distinction; Natalie is on her way to completing 18 years; and Esther has recently completed 15 years, with retirement simply not permitted. The Back Office Team throughout Overlook's history has defined consistency and dedication.

- Quarterly Reports cover portfolio allocation and performance, provide analysis of a major holding, and discuss issues of importance.

- Semiannual Presentations cover the Overlook Model, the current investment, geopolitical and macroeconomic environments, review the largest holdings in the portfolio, and provide quantitative analysis of the portfolio, Valuations, and Performance.

- Semiannual meetings across the U.S. offer Overlook's investors an opportunity to develop a more comprehensive understanding of Overlook through face-to-face communication. Esther has never sent us to Park Avenue at 10:00 when we were scheduled to be on 5th Avenue at 9:30.

- Our website includes current and historical financial statements, performance data, legal documentation, a complete library of reports, and information about Overlook management and methodologies: 30 years of everything we have published. We don't cherry pick.

- Monthly Reports include financial statements, portfolio performance, and a personalized return statement, along with Overlook's balance sheet and capital-weighted returns for each investor.

IV. Overlook's Cultural DNA

As described in the later chapter on ESG investing, my colleagues at Overlook represent one of the most stable and diverse investment management and back office teams in Asia. While diversity introduces complexity, it adds richness to our analysis and enhances our decision-making.

As we approach 30 years, it is clear that Overlook's culture and investment values help us attract and retain a certain type of person. All of us value the opportunity to compete in what is the most competitive market in the world. We have learned to channel this competitive spirit against outsiders, not internally. We don't believe in post-mortems or finger pointing when mistakes are made, or claiming credit when successes are achieved. We collectively own our successes and failures. James, Leonie, William and I agree that the shared journey at Overlook makes the long hours a reward rather than an inconvenience.

Dan Rupp manages the execution of the investment process and is an integral part of creating the culture at Overlook. He lifts the mood on volatile days and cares about the entire group of colleagues. In this effort he is supported by Angela Wang, Peck Lim Tan and Jason Lin. This fourth generation at Overlook constantly amazes the Investment Committee with their talent, dedication and enthusiasm.

One success story may be illustrative of the type of culture we hope to create. In New York City, in the early 1980s, I lived in Greenwich Village above a Korean grocer for about three years. I would like to think that I was working pretty hard in those days, but I never managed to leave for the office before Mr. Kang opened or get home from work after he had closed. And his produce was the freshest, his shelves were the best stocked, and his prices were the lowest. His dedication and hard work put all the other grocers in the neighborhood on competitive notice.

Overlook's culture encourages us to operate with dedication and purpose similar to Mr. Kang's, and with the goal of successfully competing with other fund managers at every step along the way.

- We select our company visits for more intentional purpose than others.

- We try to be better prepared for meetings.

- We strive for more insightful analysis of all our investments.

- We try to understand a company's cash flow with more insight.

- We bring our contrarian attitudes to work more effectively than our competitors.

- We execute trades a bit more carefully.

- We build deeper relationships by sending thank you notes after every single visit.

One can never tell which of these specific attributes will add to our performance in any particular year, but over time they have all made invaluable contributions.

V. Transition of Ownership at Overlook

Thirty-seven years ago, shortly after I arrived in Hong Kong, Robert Meyer, my boss at the time, described, in almost mythical terms, a lawyer he had worked for at Coudert Brothers, the preeminent American law firm in Asia at that time. The lawyer's name was Barry Metzger. So I knew of Barry for almost 15 years before I reached out to him directly for assistance in a tussle I had in Korea with Taekwang and its CEO, Ho-jin Lee, which is described in our chapter on Modern Finance Technology. Barry had passion and skills for so many things within the legal profession, but one of his main passions was corporate governance in Asia. When I reached out for help in Korea, I was fortunate that he answered my call.

It was ten years later, in 2010, that I called Barry, then a partner at Baker McKenzie in Washington, D.C. I told Barry: "I am thinking of undertaking a transition of the ownership at Overlook. I am 55 and if we are to do this correctly, it seems like we should start now. Could you recommend a lawyer who could help me work through this task?" Barry said, "Richard, give me 24 hours." Twenty-four hours later, Barry called me back and said, "Richard, I'd like to do this work, but I have two conditions: First, there is no preconceived notion of what the final solution looks like; and second, there is no preconceived timeline as to when the work will be completed." While neither Barry nor I had ever undertaken a transition of ownership, I knew for Barry it was just another puzzle to solve. So began one of the most interesting, thoughtful and rewarding years of my life.

Barry and I set out on a journey of discovery in complete privacy. He and I met in San Francisco; we met secretly in Hong Kong; we met in D.C. and New York; we had long conversations on the phone from all parts of the world at all hours of the day. I remember that early on in the process Barry said to me, "Go home and tell Dee that you are now retired. See how that feels for a week or so." I came back ever more excited about reaching our goal of keeping Overlook alive. Retirement was just not for me, nor was it for Dee. The magic of Barry Metzger was in full display throughout our year-long project.

The goal was to transition the ownership at Overlook to the next generation of leaders to achieve long-term sustainability. Barry and I carried out a comprehensive review of Overlook and our future. We realized early on that a vibrant, sustainable Overlook is worth more to all constituents than sold to an industry buyer. We formed components of the Transition after debating alternatives, taking into consideration the long-term future of Overlook beyond the second generation of ownership to third and fourth generation.

Rather than describe the Transition Plan myself, I will let Mike Lonergan, Overlook's CFO at that time, describe it from his perspective.

MIKE LONERGAN'S THOUGHTS ON THE MANAGEMENT TRANSITION

The Plan was revealed to the management team on a Monday morning in Hong Kong. Richard had been working on this for over 12 months and none of us were aware that it had been in process. Barry and Richard were very well prepared and presented the case such that it was clear they felt the offer was a once-in-a-lifetime opportunity—which, indeed, turned out to be the case.

Barry and Richard had two conditions. Everyone was in or everyone was out, and the documents needed to be signed within a month. The Transition Plan was something of a shock to the management team; but once we had time to fully consider the opportunity and its implications, we all embraced it.

The final plan is structured to achieve four goals:

1. To provide continuity of management for the benefit of the Overlook investors.

2. To recognize the contributions of the management team.

3. To create a long-term incentive for the management team to execute the Investment Philosophy and Business Practices of Overlook.

4. To reaffirm Richard Lawrence's commitment to provide leadership.

In hindsight, the Transition Plan, which Richard recognized as being necessary, achieved a goal that many investment firms fail to grasp: it established a sustainable succession plan in a timely manner. It also established its place as a core component of the Overlook Business Practices.

The Plan provided a mechanism for the gradual transfer of ownership of the business. The difficulties associated with such an endeavor should not be underestimated.

My only regret is that in 2012, a year after completing the Transition, Barry Metzger passed away too soon from pancreatic cancer. I only take comfort in knowing that Barry would be pleased with the success, duration and strength of the work we completed. We are proud to have him as a member of the Overlook Hall of Fame, albeit posthumously.

VI. ESG Investing

The subject of ESG investing at Overlook has been a natural component of our Investment Philosophy and Business Practices throughout our history. Our commitment to ESG is described in detail later in this book in the chapter entitled "ESG: The Climate Divergence."

VII. Overlook's Modern Finance Technology

Superior companies, no less than investment firms, must also implement effective business practices to deliver results to shareholders. Blind spots in a company's business practices, particularly in matters of corporate governance and capital management, can impede that delivery. At Overlook, we believe that we have a fiduciary duty to provide strategic advice to the executives of our holdings on these matters. Our objective is to help good companies become great companies.

Discussions with management have proven to be helpful to all parties – so much so that Overlook has formalized the practice under the name of Modern Finance Technology, or MFT, which we describe in a chapter later in this book.

At Overlook, we believe that superior performance is not a matter of luck or timing, but is a business objective that can be consistently achieved with methodical execution.

In these chapters we have described how our Investment Philosophy guides us to generate superior investment returns and how our Business Practices, and particularly the legal Cap on Subscriptions, are coordinated to deliver superior investment returns to Overlook's investors. The necessity to align the two cannot be overemphasized.

In the following chapter, we will describe how the confluence of the Overlook Investment Philosophy and Business Practices can nearly guarantee delivery of outperformance with the Margin of Safety for Investors.

The Overlook
Margin of Safety

A portfolio can be set up to withstand 99 percent of all scenarios but succumb because it's the remaining 1 percent that materializes. Based on the outcome, it may seem to have been risky, whereas the investment might have been quite cautious.

Another portfolio may have been structured so that it will do very well in half the scenarios and very poorly in the other half. But if the desired environment materializes and it prospers, onlookers can conclude that it was a low-risk portfolio.

— HOWARD MARKS,
The Most Important Thing

EVERY INVESTOR WISHES to outperform the market. In some years they may; in others, they may not. "That's just the market," one often hears. "Chalk it up to good luck or bad luck." "Hope for the best next year, right?"

We disagree. We believe that outperformance can and should be achieved methodically, consistently, and reliably over extended periods of time.

Let us explain.

For nearly a century, famous investors from Graham & Dodd to Warren Buffett to Seth Klarman have used the phrase "Margin of Safety" to describe the core principles that investors should strive to secure. The mere words, "margin of safety," hint at its meaning; but a precise, universal definition has always been elusive. Every investor, it seems, discusses the term differently, and perhaps that is the point: the Margin of Safety is best defined by each investor's own circumstances, experiences and skill sets.

Over the past three decades since founding Overlook, we have struggled to articulate what exactly Margin of Safety means for us. As a result, we have spoken about it infrequently and always with slight trepidation. It took us time to appreciate that the Margin of Safety is not an abstract concept, but the natural and obvious outcome of the methods we employ to achieve and deliver outperformance for investors. Today, better late than never, we offer the following definition:

> The Overlook Margin of Safety is the ability to consistently and reliably deliver superior investment returns to investors through the confluence of our Investment Philosophy and our Business Practices. This is the final result of The Overlook Model.

I. The Overlook Investment Philosophy

Earlier in Part Two, we described the Overlook Investment Philosophy and its four core components:

I.   Superior Business

II.   Management with Integrity

III. Bargain Valuation

IV.   Long Duration

We described how Overlook's dedicated leadership team, supported by a team of talented and incentivized research analysts, works to pick stocks that meet the requirements of our Investment Philosophy.

We described how detailed financial analysis of all companies in our portfolio, all companies we investigate, and comparable industry companies informs our work objectively and factually.

We also described the Overlook Pyramid. At the top of the Pyramid reside the strong and profitable businesses, whereas at the bottom of the Pyramid exist those plentiful, low-quality businesses.

As the Investment Team at Overlook succeeds in executing the Investment Philosophy, the portfolio moves toward the top of the Overlook Pyramid.

We also showed that as the Investment Philosophy drives the portfolio to the top of the Pyramid and keeps it there, we position the portfolio to deliver time-weighted returns over our benchmark over 3-, 5-, and 10-year periods.

With two caveats.

The first caveat is that you cannot afford to badly overpay for securities. Overpayment has the effect of pulling your portfolio towards the bottom of the Pyramid and erodes the ability to outperform. The second caveat emerges as the fund grows. The portfolio will overlap increasingly with the universe, making non-correlated gains from stock picking more difficult.

In the investment world there are not a lot of guarantees, and we are proud to speak with confidence about Overlook's ability to generate outperformance over the universe. There is simply no logical or factual explanation for Overlook's 14.3% time-weighted returns beating the benchmark by 6.5 percentage points per year for nearly 30 years, other than the successful execution of the Overlook Investment Philosophy.

The following table shows outperformance of time-weighted returns over the universe.

Updated as of May 31, 2021	Time -Weighted Return	Universe	Outperformance TWR over Universe*
5 years	17.1%	15.4%	1.5%
10 years	12.7%	6.9%	5.5%
20 years	17.2%	10.2%	6.4%
Since Inception (30 Years)	14.3%	7.3%	6.5%

* Calculated by geometric compounding.

II. The Overlook Business Practices

As we explained in the Business Practices chapter, Overlook starts with a very simple goal: We aim to deliver the superior returns generated by the Investment Philosophy to the Overlook investors. Success is measured by the capital-weighted returns. When delivery of returns to our investor base became Overlook's core objective, it incentivized us to adopt many policies that stand in contrast to the investment management industry, particularly with regard to growth of assets under management.

While many of the Business Practices have contributed to Overlook's delivery of returns, there is one hero in this story: the legal Cap on Subscriptions. The Cap has allowed Overlook to deliver capital-weighted returns to the Overlook investors that nearly meet or exceed the time-weighted returns over 5, 10, 20, and 30 years.

We said that all managers who adopt Business Practices that include a Cap on Subscriptions could nearly guarantee to their investors that capital-weighted returns would meet or exceed time-weighted returns over all time periods. We don't speak lightly when we say that Overlook can nearly guarantee that the outperformance will be delivered to Overlook's investors. But there is simply no logical or factual explanation for Overlook's capital-weighted returns to have nearly met or exceeded the time-weighted returns consistently over nearly three decades, other than the execution of the Overlook Business Practices.

The following table shows capital-weighted returns over time-weighted returns.

Updated as of May 31, 2021	**Capital -Weighted Return**	**Time -Weighted Return**	**Outperformance CWR over TWR***
5 years	18.4%	17.1%	1.1%
10 years	13.3%	12.7%	0.5%
20 years	16.7%	17.2%	-0.5%
Since Inception (30 Years)	14.2%	14.3%	-0.1%

* Calculated by geometric compounding.

III. The Overlook Margin of Safety

When an investor speaks confidently about their ability to generate outperformance against the universe and then deliver the outperformance to investors, my first reaction is that this statement must be snake oil. My second thought is: How else do we explain the figures in the following table?

These figures show outperformance of capital-weighted returns over the universe.

Updated as of May 31, 2021	**Capital -Weighted Return**	**Universe**	**Outperformance CWR over Universe***
5 Years	18.4%	15.4%	2.6%
10 Years	13.3%	6.9%	5.9%
20 Years	16.7%	10.2%	5.9%
Since Inception (30 Years)	14.2%	7.3%	6.4%

* Calculated by geometric compounding.

Overlook's ability to nearly guarantee the delivery of outperformance to its investors can only be explained by the confluence of our Investment Philosophy with our Business Practices to create the Overlook Margin of Safety.

As the Investment Team discussed the Overlook Margin of Safety, Leonie and William thought the concept might be depicted as an equation. We asked Jason Lin, our crack mathematician on the Investment Team, to make an attempt at turning the Margin of Safety for Investors into an equation. Many readers will find Jason's equations in the next chapter indecipherable, but the beauty and eloquence of the equation is undeniable.

Equations:
A Component of Overlook's Success

There is nothing that can be said by mathematical symbols and relations which cannot also be said by words. The converse, however, is false. Much that can be and is said by words cannot successfully be put into equations, because it is nonsense.

— CLIFFORD TRUESDELL,
American mathematician, natural philosopher,
and historian of science

W E HAVE DESCRIBED that investing is a complex, yet methodical process. We know from experience that complexity is best served by simplification. At Overlook, we use equations for exactly this purpose. Equations, at their best, combine eloquent simplicity with the irrefutable accuracy of mathematical power.

DuPont Equation: Return on Equity

In 1912, Donaldson Brown, an explosives salesman at E.I. DuPont Company, invented the DuPont Model. It has been in wide use since the 1920s and no other equation can compete for impact on the global financial system. Nothing comes even remotely close. We are thrilled to give Mr. Brown his moment in the sun.

$$\text{ROE} = \frac{\text{Net Income}}{\text{Sales}} \times \frac{\text{Sales}}{\text{Total Asset}} \times \frac{\text{Total Asset}}{\text{Average Shareholder Equity}}$$

Valuation Equation

In addition to the DuPont Model, Overlook has always found equations an essential component of our financial analysis of companies. They help us measure factors like capital intensity, pricing power, working capital efficiency, returns on reinvested capital, and so forth.

We also use equations as a means to de-emotionalize the valuation process and to secure a benchmark to judge the relative attraction of a stock, both at a specific time and over time.

Below are two valuation equations that are Overlook favorites. We discovered them buried in some of our most loved investment books. They were created in different eras, but both give investors insights into relative valuation of stocks within a universe and stocks within a portfolio.

$$\text{Ben Graham's Equation: P/B} \times \text{P/E} < 22.5$$

$$\text{John Neff's Equation: } \frac{\text{E.P.S. Growth Rate + Dividend Yield}}{\text{P/E}}$$

The Overlook Equation

In 1983, I created the original version of The Overlook Equation when comparing the relative attraction of Pep Boys: Manny, Moe and Jack, a stock I followed at J. Bush & Co., to other specialty retailers. The Equation nicely combined the core components of stock picking: profitability, growth and valuation. It has allowed Overlook to benchmark new ideas for entry into the portfolio for many decades.

Here is the original Overlook Equation:

$$\text{P/E Ratio} < \frac{\text{Return on Equity + E.P.S. Growth}}{4}$$

Over the past decades, as interest rates fell and financial analysis got more sophisticated, the Equation became outdated, despite its role being to compare relative value among stocks. Recently, we learned that Ben Graham updated his equation with each edition of *Intelligent Investor.* So, if Mr. Graham can update his equation, we decided that we could update The Overlook Equation.

Accordingly, Dan Rupp, Peck Lim Tan and I debated how we could improve the original version from nearly 40 years ago. The goal was to combine the same three critical components of stock picking: profitability, growth and valuation, but to do so in a more useful manner for today's low interest rate environment. We present, for the first time, the revised Overlook Equation:

$$\frac{\text{Normalized E.P.S. Growth Rate} + \text{Operating Return}}{\text{P/E Ratio}} = \text{Value Score}$$

The Overlook Margin of Safety Equation

We have developed three equations to describe the logical interaction of: first, our Investment Philosophy; second, our Business Practices; and lastly, the confluence of the two to create the Overlook Margin of Safety.

The combination of the three equations is the first mathematical depiction of Margin of Safety we have encountered. For simple beauty and logic, the three equations rank up there with the best.

I. THE OVERLOOK INVESTMENT PHILOSOPHY EQUATION

$$f(IP) \supseteq f(TofP \,|\, V,S) = \left\{ p \in P : R_{p,t} > R_t \, \forall t \in \{3,5,10\} \right\}$$

This equation can be read as steps in a process: The path starts with a solid Investment Philosophy (IP), supported by a creative and talented team of investors that drives the portfolio to the top of the Overlook Pyramid (TofP). Subject to maintaining a close eye on both Valuation (V) and Size (S), the top of the Pyramid delivers outperformance of the portfolio ($R_{p,t}$) over the universe (R_t) over 3-, 5-, and 10-year periods.

1. *IP*   The Overlook Investment Philosophy

2. *TofP*   Top of Pyramid: concentrate the portfolio in companies at the top of the Pyramid, but always with reference to:

   - V   Valuations: Don't badly overpay for stocks.

   - S   Size of Fund: Excessive AUM overly correlates returns to the universe.

3. $R_{p,t}$ Time-weighted return of portfolio p over a t-period

4. R_t Average return of the universe over a t-period

II. THE OVERLOOK BUSINESS PRACTICES EQUATION

$$f(BP) \supseteq f(ConS) = \left\{ p \in P : R_{p,t}^{CW} \geq R_{p,t} \; \forall t \in \{3,5,10\} \right\}$$

Then, Overlook's goal of delivering returns to the investor is embedded in our Business Practices (BP) and leads to the adoption of the legal Cap on Subscriptions (ConS). The Cap, in turn, nearly guarantees that Overlook investors' capital-weighted returns ($R_{p,t}^{CW}$) will meet or exceed the outperformance created by the Investment Philosophy Equation ($R_{p,t}$) over 3-, 5- and 10-year periods (CWR ≥ TWR).

1. *BP*   The Overlook Business Practices

2. *ConS*   The Overlook Cap on Subscriptions

3. $R_{p,t}^{CW}$ Capital-weighted return of portfolio p over a t-period

III. THE OVERLOOK MARGIN OF SAFETY EQUATION

The confluence of the Overlook Investment Philosophy and Business Practices creates the Overlook Margin of Safety: the ability to generate outperformance over the universe and nearly guarantee delivery of this outperformance to investors over 3-, 5-, and 10-year periods. The Margin of Safety for Investors is eloquently depicted below:

$$\textbf{\textit{Investment Philosophy:}}\ f(IP) \supseteq f(TofP\,|\,V,S) =$$
$$\{p \in P : R_{p,t} > R_t\ \forall t \in \{3,5,10\}\}$$

$$+$$

$$\textbf{\textit{Business Practices:}}\ f(BP) \supseteq f(ConS) =$$
$$\{p \in P : R_{p,t}^{CW} \geq R_{p,t}\ \forall t \in \{3,5,10\}\}$$

$$=$$

$$\textbf{\textit{Margin of Safety:}}\ f(IP) \cap f(BP) \supseteq f(TofP\,|\,V,S) \cap f(ConS) =$$
$$\{p \in P : R_{p,t}^{CW} \geq R_{p,t} > R_t\ \forall t \in \{3,5,10\}\}$$

Understanding these equations is fairly straightforward. Capturing the benefits of the equations requires the adoption of a clearly articulated Investment Philosophy and aligned Business Practices. Unite both together in harmony, suppress greed, start work early, end work late, give the best of all of your technical and personal skills, always stay the course, and then… you are on the path to outperformance.

Businesses can also be viewed through the lens of the Overlook Margin of Safety Equation. A company's superior business creates value, and that value must be delivered to shareholders by effective corporate governance and capital management. A superior business alone does not necessarily make a great investment if blind spots in its business practices fail to deliver results to investors. At Overlook, we assist companies in overcoming those blind spots by utilizing Overlook's Modern Finance Technology, as discussed in the following chapter.

Modern Finance Technology

It infuriates me to be wrong when I know I'm right.

— MOLIÈRE

From Confrontation to Conversation: Corporate Governance in Asia

IN PREVIOUS CHAPTERS we explained how Overlook creates outperformance over the universe by investing in superior businesses through our Investment Philosophy, as well as how Overlook delivers that value to our investors through our Business Practices.

Excellent performance and a delivery system go hand in hand. One without the other is not enough.

There are times when great companies with superior businesses have a blind spot that inhibits their ability to deliver value to shareholders. That blind spot almost always involves failings of corporate governance and capital management. In select cases, where the potential gains in

121

performance and duration justify the time and effort, Overlook will offer advice to companies to correct such shortcomings. We do so in a unique form of activism that we call Modern Finance Technology, or MFT.

MFT emerged after years of hard lessons learned. This chapter starts with a few stories of activism from the days before we figured out that MFT could achieve success in Asia.

A Concise Definition of Corporate Governance

So, what is corporate governance? Good question.

If you look it up, you may see definitions like: *Corporate governance encompasses the various administrative mechanisms, processes, procedures, and stakeholder relations by which corporations are controlled and operated.* Uh-huh. Clear as mud.

It would take some time for executives in Asia to grasp the true meaning and benefits of corporate governance and capital management, and for us to learn how to communicate our views.

A Ransacked Apartment

In the mid-1980s, some three years before I founded Overlook, I was working as an investment analyst at FP Special Assets in Hong Kong. We had an investment in the shares of a Hong Kong-listed company called Tian Teck Land. Tian Teck, through a 51%-owned subsidiary, owned the Hyatt Hotel in Tsim Sha Tsui. It was a great asset, a well-regarded tourist and business hotel in a prime location on bustling, neon-festooned Nathan Road. Our Tian Teck shares were acquired at a price that we felt was significantly below the true value of the hotel and the value of its Nathan Road land. Simple enough.

Simple enough, that is, until a whistleblower alerted us to allegations of irregularities in the company's operations, including the handling of the Hyatt renovation. Suffice it to say that these were serious allegations of practices that were certainly unfair to minority shareholders and which, if true, perhaps bordered on being criminal. We related these allegations to Tian Teck's board of directors. Their only response was to brusquely dismiss us with a wave of the hand and say they had no interest in speaking with us. Well, we said, we'd prefer to resolve these issues with you privately, but if you don't wish to do so, we can speak to you publicly in an Extraordinary General Meeting of Shareholders (EGM). Go ahead, they said, we don't care. We scheduled the EGM.

Tian Teck was owned 50.01% by the Cheong family, which left the owners in absolute control, unaccountable to shareholders. They could not be voted off the Board by minority shareholders, nor could shareholders directly influence any company practices. The EGM would likely only be a forum for discomfiting public questioning and complaint.

Then came a warning. On the night before the EGM, my wife and I returned home to find our apartment ransacked. Nothing had been taken; it was just ransacked…

LESSONS LEARNED

- 50.01% ownership permits owners to be unaccountable.
- Maybe they play by different rules in Asia.
- Better locks for my apartment.

A DESERVED REWARD

In 2021, Tian Teck Land has compounded at 3.3% per year since 1991, a meager return given the prime location of the property on Nathan Road.

The Age of Confrontation

Overlook's initiatives to fight for the rights of Overlook's investors in the 1990s were often resisted, rebuffed, ignored, dismissed or laughed at, because... they could be. Asia had not yet developed adequate laws and regulations to address corporate behavior and minority shareholders' rights. There was no culture of dialogue with minority shareholders in corporate Asia at that time. As Asia grew to greater international prominence and as more investment capital entered the public financial markets, corporate governance laws simply hadn't caught up.

In 1995 we wrote:

> Overlook Investments has long considered that the development of a well-functioning and standardized set of rules and regulations covering all areas of corporate governance and securities law is critical to Asia's economic development. Unfortunately, the rules, codes, laws and procedures are often the result of temporary, politically acceptable solutions instead of real structural reform. General apathy by institutional investors to lead efforts in standing up for the rights of shareholders has not helped. Also, many corporate managers are too willing to ignore their fiduciary obligation to minority shareholders in efforts to promote their own wealth.

Minority shareholders were on the sidelines. Outspoken shareholders were seen as bothersome activists and their opinions and objectives were often seen by management as intrusive.

Tigers Don't Change their Stripes

When companies treated us unfairly as minority shareholders, it was our fiduciary obligation to defend the rights of our clients, so we acted, every time. We would not be intimidated. It is a matter of financial equity, and of principle.

In 1995 we wrote of one such experience:

> At the present time, Overlook Investments is helping lead a group
> of minority investors in taking steps that we feel are required
> to ensure that the proposed privatization of one of our holdings,
> Fountain Set (Holdings) Limited, is made at a fair and reasonable
> price and in an equitable manner.
>
> It is my objective that this affair be settled in a positive fashion and
> in a private manner. But I want to assure my investors that I will not
> warmly support the privatization of a company in our portfolio at
> 3x current year cash flow. We are buyers, not sellers, of shares at
> this valuation.
>
> Overlook has objected strenuously to a proposed buyout of
> Fountain Set's minority shareholders at a very undervalued price.
> In recent months I have spent considerable time convincing the
> directors and other interested parties to carry out the restructuring
> in a manner that benefited all shareholders equally. I am delighted
> to report that we achieved significant success in persuading the
> directors to propose a transaction that fulfills our objectives. As
> part of the agreement I reached with the company, I requested,
> and was given, three commitments by the Board of Directors. The
> results are as follows:
>
> » The directors declared that the company will be managed as a
>   partnership between management and all investors.
>
> » The directors committed to focusing on improving the per-share
>   values of the company in the future.
>
> » The directors committed to improving the quality of the
>   disclosure of the company and its prospects with the aim of
>   improving the confidence of outside investors.
>
> I believe this level of commitment by directors to minority investors
> is unusual in Hong Kong and should lead, over time, to a substantial
> re-rating of Fountain Set from its current P/E of 4.3 times estimated
> August 1996 earnings.

The process of organizing support for our position against the original buy-out proposal, and of working to press our case for a fair deal, was time consuming and difficult. We benefited from contesting a transaction where we had the moral high ground. We secured the active support of several large fund management houses in Hong Kong and utilized Hong Kong's limited securities laws to bolster our position. I prefer life without this sort of work, although I will always protect our investments when required.

TALK IS CHEAP

At the end of the day, the directors of Fountain Set reneged on their promises to Overlook, leaving us with lingering anger, no recourse, and a gnawing concern that corporate governance in Asia had a long, long way to go. We sold after a miserable six-year holding period with an IRR of −1.1%.

And Fountain Set? In 2021, the stock is below where it was in 1995.

LESSONS LEARNED

- Promises are words. Actions are real.

- Public fights tilt the odds against Overlook because management will do almost anything to never lose face.

- Revenge is a meal best served cold.

A Tug-of-War in Korea

Korea had developed its economy around the chaebol system, in which large family-owned companies were granted privileges of monopoly power and subsidized financing by the Government. These chaebols – Daewoo, Ssangyong, Hanhwa, Hanjin, and Daelim, to name just a few that flirted with bankruptcy during Korea's so-called IMF Crisis – became the engines of industrial development.

In the years following the Asian Financial Crisis, the chaebol system had outlasted its purpose; but the psychology of privilege remained, and advances to corporate governance in Korea never really had much chance. We became increasingly concerned that Korea was simply stuck in place amidst a changing world, as discussed in the following report:

> We continue to struggle with our investments in Korea and the root cause of our difficulties seems to be repeated like a bad record. While I hate to say this, I believe that corporate leadership in Korea is becoming more and more like Japan and less like the rest of Asia. We have identified tangible and quantifiable value in public companies in Korea but see absolutely no commitment on the part of the owners to deliver any of the value to minority shareholders. This inability to adopt even a modicum of corporate governance reform makes most Korean value stocks, value traps.
>
> The difficulty we have in Korea is that the corporate sector has almost no success stories and almost no proven corporate governance leadership, especially among leading companies. Korean managers like to tell foreign investors that newly established holding companies are a sign of reform; however, my experience tells me that holding companies are just pyramid structures that permit a continuation of corporate control without accountability. Absent a significant change in the attitudes of corporate leaders, I suspect that value stocks in Korea will remain value traps. We will continue to search Korea for ideas, but my guess is that our Korean exposure will remain low.

The following story is a case in point.

TAEKWANG INDUSTRIAL

Overlook initially purchased shares in Taekwang Industrial in 1992. At that time Taekwang was one of the largest synthetic fiber producers in South Korea. It was a formidable company, going from strength to strength, and became in 1993 the strongest of our Korean investments and the second largest holding in our portfolio.

Taekwang was founded by one of the giants of the Asian textile industry, Mr. Lee Im-yong, a larger-than-life character who ran Taekwang in a manner unlike that of any other major business leader in Korea.

He was a non-conformist in a culture that admires conformity. I remember a day in 1994 when I was in Ulsan, Korea, visiting Taekwang's massive investment into a new production facility. During a visit to the office, I noticed a Mercedes-Benz sitting out in front of the entrance. You have to understand that it was practically a crime in Korea at that time not to buy a Korean vehicle, so this car caught my eye. It was Mr. Lee's car. He would drive any kind of car he wanted. No one had anything on Mr. Lee. That was one of the reasons his company had no debt. He had the confidence and independence of one who knows how to succeed.

Just as he disliked debt, he also disliked paying taxes. Mr. Lee was the most aggressive depreciator of any executive I have ever encountered in Asia. He minimized reported profits to minimize taxes, using the cash savings to avoid debt. He liked it that way. I accepted the hidden earnings and complex financial accounts because I could do my homework, even with audited financial statements only available in the Korean language. I knew he was a good executive, I knew that Taekwang was a good company, and the stock performed terrifically for Overlook.

Then, Mr. Lee died. Control of Taekwang passed to his son, Ho-jin Lee. Upon becoming CEO, poor Ho-jin, suffering from a bad inferiority complex, was immediately challenged by the 1997/98 Asian Crisis. The deep economic recession hurt Taekwang and the stock got hammered, like all stocks in Korea. Despite that, we still believed in the company that the elder Mr. Lee had built and hoped that we could help guide his son to success as economies recovered.

From 1997–2000, during and after the Asian Financial Crisis, we repeatedly discussed corporate governance and capital management with Ho-jin Lee and his management team, calling for greater transparency of the financial statements, a moderation of policies understating true earnings, and payment of dividends. Without these steps, the share price would continue to languish. Ho-jin Lee and the yes men that surrounded him always nodded, said they appreciated our advice, and sent us on our way.

By 2000, with still no concrete action by management and with no upward movement in the stock, our patience with Taekwang wore thin. Do we sell, or can we force the company to act responsibly and change dead-end policies to achieve a better share price? Taekwang made the decision for us: Ho-jin Lee, heir to his father's company but not his ability nor strength of character, crossed a red line and undertook a blatantly unfair related party transaction. We acted.

From our December 2000 report:

> Our most recent, but by no means our only, action on defending the fiduciary interests of the Overlook investors occurred recently when we hired a shareholder rights lawyer in Korea to communicate our views to the directors of Taekwang Industrial Company in a more forceful manner.
>
> This formal step was triggered by the acquisition of a commercial building from a life insurance company owned by the controlling shareholder's family, a flagrant transfer of wealth from Taekwang to offset the family's losses in the insurance business. This acquisition took place less than two weeks after two members of the senior management team assured my lawyer and me during a meeting in Seoul that no such transactions would be undertaken.
>
> Specifically, we are requesting that the directors implement a number of specific actions:
>
> » Reverse the acquisition of the commercial building.

» Initiate a policy of paying significant cash dividends.

» Execute a series of share splits to promote more active trading in the shares.

» Establish an Investor Relations department with the full support of the directors.

» Appoint additional directors who are truly independent.

The cash cost to Taekwang of these measures is small, yet our demands are enormously symbolic, particularly in a country where cash dividends of any magnitude are uncommon and the rights of management are entrenched in the law.

We are realistic about our eventual chance of success with Taekwang. Blocking our way is a culture that struggles to accept reform and political leadership that is hesitant to push reforms too quickly for fear of toppling a large number of corporates into bankruptcy.

We proposed a shareholder resolution in 2001 to elect my lawyer in Korea as an "outside auditor," which is very similar in function to an outside director, and would give shareholders accountability in company affairs. The key to the resolution was a loophole dictating that, under Korean law, the controlling Lee family could not vote. It was truly a vote of minority shareholders. All we needed was 51% of the vote of minorities. Literally days before the vote, Taekwang, sensing shareholder revolt, realized that they might well lose. Then, through either coincidence or incompetence, the largest internationally managed Korean fund cast the deciding vote against us. We found this particularly galling. Ironically, the Korean fund had been victimized more than nearly every other foreign investor by corporate governance abuses in Korea. It was an undeserved loss for Overlook, for all minority shareholders, and ultimately, for Korea.

A week later I was in my Duddell Street office in Central Hong Kong and I received a call from Overlook's lawyer in Korea who informed me that an official of the Government of Korea, unhappy with our nonconformist advice, had asked him to pass along the message that Mr. Lawrence was no longer welcome to come back to Korea. I told my lawyer to tell the official that, as an investor, Overlook no longer had any interest in returning to Korea anyway!

LESSONS LEARNED

- Korea closes ranks against foreign investors more than any other country in Asia.

- Don't rely on other minority shareholders to act logically or in alignment with our interests.

- We can't reform executives who do not understand corporate governance and capital management.

- Never run for public office in Korea.

JUSTICE PREVAILS

About 10 years ago, Bill Duke, a client of Overlook, was in Seoul meeting business partners involved in his animal trap business. He faxed me a newspaper article that described how Ho-jin Lee had been convicted of defrauding Taekwang and was pleading the court for leniency. What made Ho-jin so especially deserving of vilification was that his scheme to defraud Taekwang ended up convicting his mother as well! Now, as I write in 2021, Ho-jin is still fighting to stay out of jail a third time for other corporate crimes. Well deserved.

We sold our position in Taekwang generating an IRR of −15.6%. Today, perhaps as one might anticipate, Taekwang's share price is near a multi-decade low.

REFORM OR BE LEFT BEHIND

In the aftermath of Taekwang, I had the following to say about corporate governance in Asia:

> At Overlook, I spend a lot of my time attempting to encourage, cajole, threaten, and hound managements of all our companies to elevate the visibility of minority shareholders. My work in this area is not new, as I have been deeply involved in the protection of minority rights for the past 16 years. My aim is to anticipate mistakes before they are made and promote fair alternative solutions to business problems. While often I can be seen as a negative influence, even a disruptive force, I believe that the honesty and consistency of Overlook's advice becomes difficult to ignore over time. While clear-cut successes are too infrequent for us, we have developed thick skin, a Pitbull-like determination, and a track record of not going away.

> Thankfully, as I look across Asia, the direction of reform and the ultimate success of reform are no longer in doubt. President Estrada of the Philippines is on the brink of being impeached. Thaksin Shinawatra, the leading candidate for president of Thailand, looks likely to be ruled ineligible to hold public office for five years due to illegal nondisclosure of his wealth. And Jason Chang, President of ASE, a major electronic company in Taiwan, is on his way to jail for six years for fraudulent business dealings. These events could not have occurred 15 years ago, maybe even seven years ago. They reflect new openness, new accountability, and are the result of years of steady, often unnoticed, reform. Yes, more needs to be accomplished, but the direction is set.

Modern Finance Technology

As Asian economies developed, corporate governance was increasingly accepted by authorities and corporations as necessary to Asia's competitive success.

Here is an excerpt from our December 2000 report:

> The benefits of corporate governance and capital management are direct and immediate for us as investors. We believe that every company in Overlook's portfolio could improve returns to us by improving business practices. We also believe that improved minority shareholder protections are a critical component to rebuilding investor confidence across Asia.

To our satisfaction, attitudes began to change. The 1997/98 Asian Crisis created an environment of massive wealth destruction in which only the strongest would survive. Companies needed to reform to succeed, and as a consequence, our advice began to be heard.

WHAT'S IN A NAME?

In order to talk about corporate governance clearly, we needed a language for it. If we called our advice "corporate governance" or "activism," we would risk losing the trust of executives from the start. So, we called it Modern Finance Technology. It has a nice ring to it, and it is uniquely Overlook.

Modern, because all executives want to be up to date with the latest. *Finance*, because finance is crucial to every company, and every executive wants to learn more about it. *Technology*, because executives understand the need to embrace the benefits of today's advancing technology, in every sense of the word.

Put together, the term *Modern Finance Technology* is the perfect phrase that allows us to engage senior executives to resolve blind spots.

We formally defined Modern Finance Technology as follows:

> The provision of conflict-free and private advice to owners and CEOs from the perspective of a long-term shareholder on capital management and corporate governance to enhance the long-term value of the corporation. We help build better public companies.

Branded as Modern Finance Technology, executives began leaning in to learn about our approach, and for the last 20 years MFT has been a major contributor to Overlook's and our companies' success.

Our MFT experiences with two companies, Chroma ATE and CP All, showed how much our world had changed by the early 2000s.

Chroma ATE: Resistance, Then Acceptance

In the mid-1990s, Overlook briefly owned shares in Chroma ATE, a Taiwan-based company that manufactures high value-added test and measurement equipment. We were attracted to the company's technology and management but became disappointed when management was reluctant to divest non-core operations. This hurt the impressive earnings of their core business and their willingness to pay cash dividends. We discussed these ideas with Chroma, but they hesitated. They just weren't yet ready to act. We sold our position at a loss.

Despite that decision we always admired Ming Chang, co-founder and executive director of Chroma, for his abilities, ethics and energy, and we stayed in touch with him in the years that followed. A few years later, in 2004, I was pleased to receive a call from Ming in my Hong Kong office. He said, "You know, Richard, you've been up here in the past talking to us about this thing called MFT, and we're beginning to understand what you've been saying all these years. We'd really appreciate it if on your next trip to Taiwan you could stop by and talk to us so we could learn about MFT." Within a week I was on a plane to Taipei.

The rest of the story is told in our March 2005 report:

> Shortly after my phone call, with the stock near an all-time low, I met with Ming Chang to discuss our thoughts on MFT. It did not take long to sense the profound change in attitude at Chroma on many of the specific issues that we had debated a few years earlier. Ming spoke of management's commitment to sell non-core businesses, to reduce the number of free shares given to employees, to buy back shares, to pay cash dividends, to stop investment in minority stakes in unlisted high-tech companies, and to push the return on equity above 20%.
>
> Equally important, Ming displayed optimism regarding new products that had been under development for several years. These, I quickly realized, had the potential to transform Chroma's test and measurement business from a chair with two legs to one with five. Overlook also discovered that the construction of Chroma's large new office and research center was nearing an end, with few other capex requirements in sight. Shortly after Ming and I spoke, Overlook began an accumulation of Chroma stock.
>
> Companies that grasp all aspects of corporate governance and operate superior businesses have generated the bulk of Overlook's gains over the past six years. In the case of Chroma, I have never doubted that they run an excellent technology-based business.
>
> Ming and his co-founder, Leo Chin Ming Huang, "get it," and this is what re-rating of P/Es is all about. The shares have, in the short time since, risen nearly 30% from our average cost.

THE COST OF IMPATIENCE

We sold Chroma after 6.1 years generating a 31.5% IRR. Today the stock is sitting near a multi-decade high. Our mistake was reacting to a short-term overvaluation, neglecting to consider the value of executives who understand the "secret sauce."

LESSONS LEARNED

- Never lose sight of a superior business.

- Relationships with executives, built over time, open the door to MFT.

- Hesitate twice before selling a MFT graduate.

A Win-Win at CP All

Overlook has always been interested in the convenience store industry. The industry is typified by some of our favorite qualities: consistent growth, stable margins, negative working capital, high rates of return on operating assets, and high generation of free cash flow. For those reasons, however, these businesses are often too richly priced for Overlook.

We nevertheless followed the industry closely, and our interest was piqued in 2004 by a Thai company called CP All, which owned the world's fourth-largest 7-Eleven chain. It controlled slightly over 50% of market share and serviced over four million Thai customers every day. If ever there were a tollbooth on Thailand's economy, CP All would be it.

ONE RED FLAG

There was, however, a red flag of caution in CP All's business: a 29.7% interest in the Lotus Supercenter, the third largest hypermarket operator in East China. We expected to find a profitable convenience store business and a massive black hole in the Lotus operation, but were surprised to find that Lotus was, for the time being, profitable. Because most investors were put off by the Lotus business, the share price was, in our view, undervalued, and Overlook was able to acquire CP All shares at an attractive price.

As we developed a working relationship with CP All management, we expressed our opinion that if the Lotus stake was spun-off, investors would embrace CP All with a higher share price reflecting the true value of the core business. Management hesitated; but in 2005, when the Lotus business turned unprofitable, our advice was heard.

MODERN FINANCE TECHNOLOGY: OVERLOOK'S ROLE IN RESTRUCTURING CP ALL

In 2007, after 18 months of discussion and hard work, the Lotus divestment was completed, as told in our June 2007 report:

> Every few years we have a success at Overlook that makes all the long hours, headaches, and challenges of stock picking for a living really worthwhile. In the second quarter we had one such event.
>
> On May 18 CP All announced a major restructuring that will result in the separation of their unprofitable Lotus hypermarket business in China from their 7-Eleven business in Thailand. We had argued in favor of this with directors and senior managers of the CP Group over the previous 18 months.
>
> Many investment managers can and will claim today that they foresaw the need for the separation of Lotus from CP All. However, the involvement of Overlook has been particularly deep in this respect. We did extensive research to figure out a step-by-step process so that the CP Group could complete its cross-border transaction. This involved building trust within top management and owners of the CP Group, whose chairman, Khun Dhanin Chearavanont, committed time and effort to fully understand Overlook's vision for CP All.

Overlook made multiple presentations to ensure management stayed focused on the ultimate long-term objective. It required tremendous conviction on our part as we watched the hypermarket business in China lose profitability over the past 12 months. And it took patience to give the various parties time to get all their ducks lined up. Would this transaction have happened without Overlook? Probably. Would it have been completed in such a manner that it was a win-win for every party, including minority shareholders? Probably not.

Two major positives have already come out of the reorganization. First, CP All's share price rose 61% in the last quarter and has put on another 22% so far in June, providing us with some welcome gains. Second, and vastly more important, our ultimate objective has been realized. CP All is part of a small fraternity of superior businesses in Asia which Overlook hopes to own for the next three to seven years.

LESSONS LEARNED

- Make your appeals personal and your advice correct.

- Move the company from 12:00 to 1:30, and then let great executives move their companies from 1:30 to 6:00 as the benefits of Overlook's advice are realized.

- Superior businesses are always worth fighting to fix.

A MATCH MADE IN HEAVEN

Infrequently during investment careers, opportunities present themselves that allow an investor to generate lifelong record returns. Our investment in CP All, which spanned from 2004 to 2013, was just such an investment. The business was exactly what we strive to uncover. We bought it right, we helped majority owners and management restructure the business for all the correct motivations, and we sold it at the right price at the appropriate time. In doing so, CP All, Khun Dhanin and his family, the executives and many workers earned a spot very close to Overlook's heart.

The numbers today are still stunning. We invested US$ 38 million and made profits of US$ 333 million, generating an IRR for Overlook of 48.5% over the 8.4-year holding period. It was a match made in heaven and a ride that we all thoroughly enjoyed.

How to Do It Right

With the positive experiences we had with Chroma and CP All, the benefits of Overlook's Modern Finance Technology were clear. Each successful implementation of MFT served as an example for other companies to follow suit.

From our September 2005 report:

> In the past months certain events have unfolded that have made me realize change is beginning to happen in Asia that portends good days ahead for Overlook's investors. Allow me to share my opinion as to why public companies are suddenly embracing Overlook's advice:
>
> » The reward for getting corporate governance correct has never been higher and companies are recognizing this. I often used to say before 1997 that "good corporate governance and a dollar will get you a cup of coffee." Well, the Economic Crisis of 1997/98 changed a lot of this and the reward for good behavior is evident and large.
>
> » CEO awareness of the power and value of Overlook's conflict-free advice has soared. Properly aligned advice is a rare commodity in Asia, and CEOs are finally realizing this. Overlook's policy of watching before advising, listening before speaking, and talking privately and confidentially is being increasingly acknowledged. This is typified by comments from

many CEOs who tell us they haven't heard Overlook's advice from anyone else in the financial community.

» I have always wanted Overlook to be "top of mind" when a CEO thought of minority shareholders. Well, Overlook has never been closer to achieving that elusive goal. Without a doubt this position will assist us in maintaining an open and honest discussion of important issues with our company managers.

WHERE DOES THIS LEAD US?

As in the past, my preference is to invest in the companies of this world whose managements seldom need advice or anything more than a polite and sincere "thank you." But the world is not a perfect place yet. As Walter Schloss, a well-regarded value investor and a notable disciple of Ben Graham, once said prophetically, "you never know a stock until you own it." This is always the case with our holdings. But what is happening now is that Overlook is increasingly in a position to positively influence outcomes.

There are, however, a few rules Overlook must respect:

» Overlook must establish a relationship of trust with the company in advance of providing MFT advice. This takes time.

» Corporate executives must have confidence that our discussions will remain private and confidential.

» Overlook waits at least a year after meeting a company to make MFT recommendations. Management has to understand we are not short-term investors pursuing short-term gains.

» We must approach management only after proper and thorough consideration has been given to all issues.

» Management must feel that our MFT advice is free of conflicts of interest, which cannot always be said about recommendations from mid-level executives, family members, brokers, or particularly investment bankers.

» We must meet one-on-one, face to face. Two people in the room can lead to success. Ten people in the room will lead to nothing.

» We rely only on Overlook, not on outsiders or other minority shareholders, to provide MFT advice.

Making Great Companies Even Better

Overlook's Modern Finance Technology has come a long way, from having one's apartment ransacked in the early days to successfully influencing change at some of the best companies in Asia.

The story of MFT's increasing relevance and acceptance mirrors the story of Asia's economic advancement over the past 30 years. At Overlook, we are pleased to have been there through it all, and gratified that our work has played at least some small part in making great companies even better.

PART THREE

Overlook in China from 1985 to 2021

不争论，是为了争取时间干。

Not arguing is to buy more time for real work.

WHILE THE STORY of Asia over the past four decades has been dominated by China, it is important to remember that China's story is the story of all of Asia. Indeed, the rise of Asian economies began earlier, in most areas of Asia *except* China, when Asia's smaller countries were dynamos of entrepreneurial activity.

This book is not intended to be just another China book. It is about investing in a region that has undergone dramatic and historic change. But our experiences in China reflect the ways that Overlook's methods of investing have succeeded while Asia grew and matured over the past three decades.

In the following chapters we will tell of Overlook's experiences in China during three distinct periods:

1. Chasing Rainbows: China 1985–2000

2. We Don't Invest in China Because China… Is China: 2000–2013

3. The Hunt: China 2013–2021

Overlook's experience in China has variously been frustrating, fascinating, annoying and uplifting, but ultimately, exciting and rewarding.

We'll start in 1985. I had just arrived in Hong Kong as a young analyst and Asian equity markets sometimes seemed to me like the lawless Wild West. Just a few miles away from my office in Hong Kong, across the border in Guangdong Province, Deng Xiaoping's Open Door Policy was quietly beginning to stir change. At first this was hardly noticeable to many and was merely a hint of all that was to come.

Chasing Rainbows:
China: 1985–2000

改革是中国的第二次革命, 这是一件必须做的事, 尽管是有风险的事。

Reform is China's second revolution. It's something that must be done, albeit risky.

— DENG XIAOPING

Humble Beginnings

IN EARLY 1985, just months after I had arrived in Hong Kong, I met with Dennis Ting, CEO of Kader Industrial, at the company's factory. It was located in an aging industrial building in Aberdeen, on the south shore of Hong Kong Island.

The company was founded by Dennis' father, who was part of the generation that had fled China in 1949 and energized post-war Hong Kong with entrepreneurial spirit. By the mid-1980s, Kader, now under Dennis' leadership, had grown into a respected toy manufacturer and exporter with products including Star Wars figurines, Teddy Ruxpin and Cabbage Patch Kids.

147

After our meeting, in a parting conversation while I waited for the factory elevator, Dennis mentioned that the company had started doing some simple component manufacturing in small villages across the Hong Kong border in Guangdong Province, where Dennis and the Kader management team had relatives. "They work hard, out of basic factories," he said, "and wages are really low up there. Interesting possibilities."

Asia was at the starting gate. Could there be a better place to live and work?

Early Days in Asia: Not So Fast, Rookie

I arrived in Hong Kong with three years' experience as a security analyst in New York. I had researched solid, professionally managed companies like Liz Claiborne, clothes for the working woman; Multimedia Inc., monopoly TV and radio stations in the Southeast; Tandon Corp., maker of the first floppy disc drive for the IBM PC Junior; and Brown Group, a retailer of branded footwear. I made a few mistakes, but generally American companies follow the rules of the road.

Then, in 1986, I started investing in Asia. It was another world. I was welcomed in December 1985 by the PanEl Crisis when the Singapore and Malaysian stock markets closed for three days due to the debt default of the high-flying Pan-Electric Industries and the threatened collapse of Promet Holdings, another Southeast Asian momentum stock of those days. Odd, I thought, to close the whole exchanges – but OK, I guess.

Slowly I realized that Hong Kong was a modern-day Wild West. Everyone kept telling me to be careful. The vocabulary was different: family-controlled corporations, related party transactions, related party asset injections, rights issues, and pyramid structures. The daddy of them all was the Deep Discount Rights Issue (DDRI), a corporate manoeuvre that massively disadvantaged minority shareholders, as illustrated in the paragraphs that follow. I kept asking myself: can controlling shareholders do this to minority shareholders?

In terms of cleverness, insidiousness and pure criminality, nothing can compare to the DDRI. It was perfected by Joseph Lau of Evergo Industrial, a manufacturer of ceiling fans. Mr. Lau correctly understood there was more money in DDRIs than in selling ceiling fans.

My classic example of the DDRI was carried out by a businessman named Poon Jing in 1991, who acquired control of FP Special Assets, a public company where I was employed, for HK$ 1.038/share in July 1991. Since FP Special Assets was closely held and we knew the reputation of Mr. Poon, we advised our shareholders to tender all their shares, with the result that he acquired 99%-plus control of the renamed Asia Orient.

The day after the FP Special Assets transaction closed, Asia Orient was the number one most traded share on the Hong Kong Stock Exchange. How could that happen? Well, Mr. Poon, it turned out, was moving shares from his right hand to his left hand to ramp up the share price. Retail punters jumped in, driving the share price even higher. Asia Orient became a "hot" stock with sexy, intoxicating rumors of future growth. Trading volume rocketed and the rising share price seduced momentum investors, and even a few international fund managers, to buy into Asia Orient. Under the DDRI methodology created by Mr. Lau, Mr. Poon distributed shares to the speculators as the shares rose.

When the stock reached HK$ 1.44/share, Mr. Poon began to distribute shares to speculators more aggressively, driving the share price down. Investors averaged down as the price dropped past HK$ 1.20/share, then past HK$ 0.80/share, all the way down until Asia Orient reached HK$ 0.50/share in February 1992. At this point the former 99.9% shareholder disclosed that he owned exactly 56.5% of Asia Orient.

Precisely as Mr. Poon had anticipated, the depressed shareholders felt Asia Orient was gum on their shoes and knowledge of their investment needed to be withheld from their spouses. Mr. Poon was now ready to execute his coup de grace. In February 1992, Mr. Poon underwrote a 2-for-1 Rights Issue at HK$ 0.27/share, triggering a further collapse of the shares to HK$ 0.30/share. Since investors couldn't stomach averaging down yet again, many, if not most, let their Rights shares lapse. Mr. Poon, therefore, was able to buy back, at HK$ 0.27/share, all of the shares he had sold at higher prices. The Deep Discount Rights Issue fleecing was now complete.

A FAILURE OF REGULATION

In a sign of the times, The Nikko Securities Co. (Asia) Limited called the Rights Issue fleecing "in the overall interests of Asia Orient" and stated, "the terms of the Rights Issue are fair and reasonable." What makes this story more painful for the poor minority shareholders is that Mr. Poon executed five more Rights Issues following the 1992 swindle and shareholders who simply held their 100 shares of FP Special Assets are down 98% in 2021. Nigerian scammers have nothing to teach Mr. Poon.

As for Mr. Lau, the mastermind, of the DDRI, he was convicted of bribery and money laundering in Macau in 2014 and sentenced to five years in jail. He remains in Hong Kong due to the lack of an extradition treaty. But his conviction came decades after he had mastered the DDRI.

Trial and Error

The first stock I ever purchased in Hong Kong, in 1986, was TVB, the monopoly TV broadcaster in Hong Kong with millions more people in Guangdong province pirating its signal. I bought TVB at 5.4 times earnings on the assumption that its owner and CEO, Sir Run Run Shaw, who was 78 at the time, would pass away in the next few years and the business would be sold. TVB was a terrific investment and Sir Run Run Shaw did pass away—28 years later, at the age of 106, just as I had envisioned.

At the same time, and as predicted by Dennis Ting, low-cost manufacturing in China caught on quickly and housing for migrants from all parts of China into Guangdong was in high demand. In 1988, while I was still working at FP Special Assets, we bought a stake in Tian An China Investments, a Hong Kong-listed company that controlled a massive swath of land in the Shenzhen Special Economic Zone, just across the Hong Kong border. It was called China Overseas Town, depicted in this photograph from 1985, and land sold for less than a tenth of prices in Hong Kong. The possibilities!

Then, on June 4, 1989, Tiananmen Square protests ended in turmoil. The owners of Tian An were on the wrong side of the politics, the big boss at First Pacific forced us to sell, and the Chinese Government eventually revoked their control of the land.

Had the company been able to keep the land, it would have created one of the great real estate fortunes in Asia. I weep when I see this photograph of China Overseas Town today.

Chasing Rainbows

Like many investors, I spent much of my time in Asia back then searching for the pot of gold at the end of every rainbow in China. Sell a toothbrush, rice cracker, or air conditioner to every Chinese citizen. Or one of anything at all. A commentator said it well: "I just want to sell one sock to everyone in China!"

Wo Kee Hong is one failed attempt at finding treasure. It was a Hong Kong-listed company that manufactured and sold air conditioners to the domestic China market. The company looked good enough on paper and we liked management, so we bought a stake. Then we arranged a visit to their factory.

It was a 20-minute taxi ride from the ferry pier in Zuhai to Jiangmen, an industrialized city in the Pearl River Delta of Guangdong Province. In just the first few blocks we noticed a factory of another air conditioner company. Then another. Then another after that. We counted five more air con manufacturers before we arrived at Wo Kee Hong; and those, Overlook realized, were most likely among hundreds of small air con companies that must have existed in Southern China at that time. All were competing against each other with the same idea, and most would soon disappear. Needless to say, Overlook found no treasure in Wo Kee Hong.

Twenty years later, when the process of Darwinian economics had finally ended, there were only three air conditioning manufacturers left standing in China. Overlook invested in one of them, an excellent company called Midea which in that short period had become one of the largest appliance manufacturers in the world.

In addition to Wo Kee Hong, we had plenty of other treasureless rainbows in those early days:

- Ultronics: Ultrasounds for every expecting mother in China.

- Wai Kee: Highways throughout China for all the prospective car owners.

- China Hong Kong Photo: Rolls of film for every aspiring Ansel Adams in the Mainland.

The experience taught me that chasing intoxicating rainbows in China was really only a disguised form of chasing greed, which inevitably disappoints.

What other way could we take advantage of China's growth?

Alphabet Soup

In the early- to mid-1990s, China began cautious attempts to open share markets with what we call the alphabet soup of public companies. A-Shares, B-Shares, H-Shares and Red-Chips were all designed to secure capital for badly run state-owned enterprises without giving up control to minority shareholders, embracing any acceptable form of corporate governance, or permitting China's private enterprises to participate. Most were just acquisition vehicles for the injection of additional low-quality state assets.

The first Chinese company to list U.S.-dollar B-Shares that foreigners could freely trade on the Shanghai Stock Exchange was Shanghai Chlor-Alkali Chemical. I have the first earnings announcement on my office wall. It is filled with typos and mistranslations. China's public companies still had a long way to go.

Speculators, however, were not put off, and China's SOEs became a roller coaster of boom, bust, and scandal. Overlook had no interest. As Wu Jinglian, the PRC economist, once said, "China's stock markets are worse than a casino. At least in a casino there are rules."

We wrote this note to the Overlook investors in 1995:

> China is prone to disappointment and continues to pose challenges to the fundamental investor. Our direct exposure to China's A-Shares, B-Shares, H-Shares and overseas listings is nil. The difficulty of finding a vehicle with earnings predictability makes investing in China an ongoing challenge. I miss the security that comes with a 10-year track record.

Factory of the World, But...

Overlook also tried an indirect route into China, by investing in profitable Hong Kong-listed manufacturing companies that were part of China becoming the "factory of the world." These vehicles offered us at least a bit of legal protection, access to management, and modest legal assurance in case we encountered disappointments. The problem was that they were generally cash flow negative, with volatile streams of revenue and profit, and had inexperienced management teams – hardly what Overlook would consider to be superior businesses.

Some of the companies that rotated through our portfolio included lesser lights such as Wong's International, IIH, QPL, Tomei, Pantronics, and Vtech. We'd buy them at 4× earnings and sell them at 6×. None of these were bad companies, but they certainly weren't great companies. They weren't Overlook companies. They didn't fit with our Investment Philosophy of identifying great, well-managed companies for long-term investment. China, for Overlook, remained a frustration.

And Then We Found Kingboard

A long road had been travelled since my meeting in 1986 with Dennis Ting, whose relatives in China assembled Kader toys in their villages. We had struggled to figure out a comprehensive business model that took advantage of business in China. Then we met Kingboard Chemical. Kingboard understood the importance of scale and vertical integration in manufacturing, but they also understood finance. Kingboard was in a league of their own.

You can hear my excitement in this discussion of Kingboard in our June 2000 report:

> Kingboard Chemical, a Hong Kong-listed entity, manufactures and sells laminates to the printed circuit board (PCB) industry, principally in Southern China. The Company controls a 40% market share in Southern China and an approximate 15% market share worldwide. Since listing in 1993, Kingboard has grown revenue and profits at compound rates of 39.6% and 42.9% respectively.

> Overlook first met the management of Kingboard Chemical shortly after their IPO. Meetings in 1995 and 1997 followed that initial encounter. Although Overlook did not buy the shares after these visits, our interest in the business and our confidence in the management grew. These meetings were complemented by routine visits to PCB houses, consumer electronics, computer and telecommunication product manufacturers around Asia. A common thread in all these meetings was the insatiable demand for lower cost raw materials and lower cost manufacturing centers. In essence, the electronics industry was being driven into Southern China, the low-cost manufacturing center in Asia if not the world.

> In November 1998, in the midst of the 97/98 Asian Crisis, I made the journey to Fotan, in the New Territories of Hong Kong, to visit with Paul Cheung and Patrick Chan, Founders of Kingboard Chemical. Unlike so many corporate executives at that time who complained of falling volumes, falling prices, and unused capacity, Paul and Patrick spoke of their business with confidence. They described steady margins, consistent volume growth, lower capex requirements, falling debt levels, and the attractive potential of the copper foil business that Kingboard was bringing online. At 3.5 times March 1999's E.P.S. estimate, it was all I needed to hear.

As we parted, Paul pulled me aside and said, "You know, Richard, you are the first investment analyst to come by in over six months. Good to see you again. Thank you."

As I exited the elevator from the 20-storey industrial building, I grabbed my first-generation Motorola mobile phone to buy our first shares. It was the beginning of our acquisition of just over 4% of the company at an average price of HK$ 1.13 or less than 2.0 times March 2000's E.P.S. While many investors could have bought shares at that time, it was our relationship with the management and our knowledge of the business that gave us the confidence to buy a big stake.

I like this tale as it reveals much about Overlook's day-to-day work in Asia. Often our investments are the culmination of years of indirect background work and the process of osmosis, whereby we accumulate insights and relationships that only pay off months or years later. This is principally why we structure so much of our research effort around company visits.

While the valuation of Kingboard at the time of our purchase was an undeniable bargain, our earlier visits had confirmed the principal attraction of this successful Asian manufacturer.

ANOTHER DAY WITH KINGBOARD CHEMICAL

I recall spending a day in early 1999 visiting various Kingboard factories in Southern China with Patrick Chan. The day was full of explanations of production processes, relations with key customers, and capex figures interspersed between hair-raising drives down rural roads criss-crossing Guangdong Province from one Kingboard factory to another. However, the most memorable moment of the day occurred as we returned, well after dark, to the Shenzhen Immigration and Border Control. There, standing along the side of the highway next to his SUV with dual license plates (Hong Kong's most meaningful status symbol), was Kingboard's Chairman, Paul Cheung. He was waiting to give us a ride across the border to Hong Kong. While I appreciated the ride, what really impressed me was

Cheung's intense enthusiasm as he updated Patrick on the day's orders and production volumes. I did not need to speak Cantonese to know this man was exhilarated about his business, absorbed in his mission, and in full partnership with Patrick.

Like most entrepreneurial companies in Asia, Kingboard reflects the risk/reward parameters of its major shareholders. Cheung is the risk taker in the Company. It was he who pushed Kingboard to keep expanding in the face of the Asian crisis. Patrick Chan is the soft-spoken, English-speaking face of the Company, quietly watching the cash flow, line-of-business profit margins, and monthly profits. They have a long history together as partners, having co-founded the Company in 1980. Since we often find CEOs that have many but not all of the requirements to be a successful CEO of a public company, we are happy to see the mix of personalities in Kingboard.

A FANTASTIC PARTNERSHIP

Kingboard Chemical remained in the Overlook portfolio for 14 years, generating an IRR of 41.1%. In a first at Overlook, three of Kingboard's executives, founders Paul Cheung and Patrick Chan, along with Chadwick Mok, CFO, are all members of the Overlook Hall of Fame.

Kingboard was a watershed investment for Overlook. The long frustration in finding true value that benefitted from the growth of China was finally resolved by Kingboard. And if Kingboard was proving successful in China, perhaps there were others out there as well. The hunt was on, and Overlook's next phase of opportunity in China began, as we describe in the following chapter.

We Don't Invest in China Because China... Is China:
2000–2013

我从来不吓唬老百姓，只吓唬那些贪官污吏。

I have never intimidated the masses... I only intimidate corrupt officials.

— ZHU RONGJI,
Premier of People's Republic of China, 1998–2003

W E BEGAN MANY chapters in this book with mistakes we have made, like chasing rainbows in China, or being swindled by Citiraya, the company in Singapore that was forever on lunch break. We have no shortage of stories about misguided investments we have made: it's part of the business, so we chalk it up to experience, have a good laugh at ourselves, and keep moving forward a little wiser each time.

The time period we will cover in this chapter is from 2000–2013. It was a new age for corporates in Asia excluding China, when a new generation of Asian companies had learned how to create long-term value. These were the companies that Overlook had long strived to identify, available now at bargain valuations following the 1997/98 Asian Crisis.

It was a time when corporate Asia ex-China had matured to a strength and momentum that fit perfectly with our Investment Philosophy, when fundamental investing found real traction for Overlook. These companies were Overlook's New Winners. They came in many flavors all across Asia ex-China, and we loved them all. A few of our favorites include:

- **Indonesia:** Bank NISP, Multi Bintang
- **Thailand:** CP All, Thai Re, Thai Union Foods
- **Malaysia:** Top Glove, IOI
- **Singapore:** MobileOne
- **Hong Kong:** Café de Coral, Kingboard Chemical, ASM Pacific
- **Taiwan:** TSMC, Advantech, Chroma ATE

Many of these companies are highlighted elsewhere in this book; their executives are in the Overlook Hall of Fame; and nearly all are in the Decade Club. Two are in the Two Decade Club.

But something else was happening in Asia, too. China's economy kept compounding at high rates of growth.

A Giant Awakens

It was breathtaking. Driven by manufacturing and exports, China's economy nearly doubled in size from 2000 to 2005, then doubled again by 2008. Hong Kong, Overlook's home and the most dynamic financial center in Asia, seemed to dwindle in comparison to China's expansion, despite terrific growth.

Hong Kong GDP as a % of China GDP

1990	21.3%
2000	14.0%
2010	3.8%
2020	2.3%

It was impossible not to be aware of what was happening in China. China was hyper-competitive globally. Even though we were busy with the New Winners across the Asian region, Overlook couldn't help but pay attention to China from our home in Hong Kong. China was becoming an economic engine on a scale that was certain to produce investment opportunities. We kept looking, visiting companies, learning about business in China, trying to figure out the best way for Overlook to invest in China.

Slowly, with a lot of work, options began to take shape. We described these developments in our December 2001 report, which includes one of the most significant sentences we have ever written:

"The emergence of 30 to 40 listed private enterprises marks the inception of what will be a long list of future listings from China's private sector."

One of the most exciting developments in Asia over the past two years has been the emergence of real public companies in China. By "real public companies," we mean companies that utilize the free-market principles to manage their businesses for profit in China. In general, these companies are majority owned and managed by dynamic, yet unproven, entrepreneurs. Their markets are large, fragmented, and offer both incredible potential rewards and enormous competitive challenges. This select group of public companies stands in stark contrast to standard Chinese public companies that have been spun off from monolithic State-Owned Enterprises (SOEs). The prime aim of SOE subsidiaries seems to be to raise capital from investors to subsidize the bloated overheads of employees and to acquire further marginal assets from the parent.

While macroeconomic data in China is suspect, official data shows that private businesses currently generate approximately 45% of the GNP of China. Yet, private enterprises comprise less than 5% of the market capitalization of Chinese stocks. So, while many of the current group of entrepreneurs and companies will disappear for a whole host of good and bad reasons, we are certain that the sector as a whole will yield dynamic growth and plenty of scary moments for investors.

For Overlook, this presents an exciting opportunity that plays to our strengths of fundamental analysis and active involvement in the research of all our investment ideas.

The Door Cracks Open

Because direct ownership of Chinese shares by foreigners was restricted in the early 2000s, Overlook's investment universe was limited to Chinese companies with overseas listings. As noted above, by the end of 2001 there were only 30 to 40 listed private enterprises. For all of China's size and growth, that's a tiny cohort of private enterprises available for investors.

While we were eager to find access to China, we could not compromise our standards to do so. Any decision to invest in China had to compare favorably with the many excellent opportunities we owned in the portfolio. As we worked our way through the list, People's Food caught our interest. (We introduced you to its capable CEO, Zhou Lian-kui, in the chapter on the Overlook Investment Philosophy.)

From our December 2001 report:

> People's Food (PF) is the largest integrated pork processor in China, with sales and profits for 2002 estimated to reach US$ 745 million and US$ 100 million respectively. The Company has four abattoir facilities across China and distributes its products through a nationwide network.

Financially, People's Food is characterized by stable margins, high asset turnover and high returns on assets. Since 1997, gross margins and operating margins have averaged 21.5% and 16.3%, respectively. In 1998, PF generated sales of Rmb 6.2 of sales per renminbi of averaged fixed assets. In 2001, we estimate PF will generate Rmb 7.5 of sales per renminbi of average fixed assets. Not many public companies in Asia have managed to improve asset turnovers when sales rose by a factor of nearly three times. As a result of steady margins and high asset turnover, the return on average operating assets has averaged a whopping 55% over the past five years. This places PF in the top quartile of companies in our portfolio and allows PF to self-finance 30%-plus growth in sales through internally generated funds. And, as I have always maintained, companies that generate excess cash tend to have fewer problems with corporate governance.

Although we have only a five-year track record for People's Food, their operating margins have been steady, reasonable and consistent with their productivity advantages. Their working capital management shows none of the abuses or lack of discipline so often seen in China. As for PF's corporate finance intentions, we have watched the Company turn away underwriting offers for placement of new shares due to their high level of cash and lack of a productive use of proceeds.

We were fortunate to come across People's Food at a very attractive time and at an attractive price. We bought our position at an average P/E of 3.9 times current year earnings, a level that made our decision relatively easy. However, we are excited about owning a company whose goal is to self-finance 30% profit growth. At the current time, the shares are still modestly priced at 7.7 times 2001's estimated E.P.S. and 6.1 times 2002's estimated E.P.S. with a 5.0% cash yield and a 48.1% return on average equity. As with every investment in Asia, and particularly China, our confidence can only be established by the steady creation of a track record of performance and honest corporate governance over time. Clearly, we are off to a good start with Mr. Zhou.

We held our shares in People's Food for almost nine years and realized an IRR of only 9.8%. However, as one of our first investments in a company that operated entirely in China, People's Food also provided us with invaluable on-the-ground insight into the challenges and opportunities of the China market. If we were presented with the same circumstances today, we would still invest in People's Food.

China... Is China

Along with our investment in People's Food, we were optimistic to find others, but China is never easy.

We spent a large percentage of our time searching for investment ideas in China. Time after time, companies and stocks that looked promising wound up in the junk heap after close scrutiny disclosed critical, often cancerous, failings. Every so often, we felt that our skepticism towards China was blocking prospective success and we needed to open our minds to the impressive future of the country. Yet company after company exposed the difficult conditions for minority shareholders within the PRC. Yes, plenty of growth, just no profits. Ridiculous expansions, too much short-term debt, unsustainable margins, "growth at all costs" management strategies, misallocation of capital, conflicts of interest between shareholder classes, 14% stakes in rural highways, and ill-timed diversifications are but a sampling of the difficulties we encountered. Rarely have we ever examined such a broad mix of companies and come up so empty-handed.

On the bright side, we became convinced that capitalism, along with animal spirits of retail investors, was alive and well in China. Capitalism comes naturally to the Chinese. But the country needed a massive "flushing of the toilet" to take away unqualified, undisciplined, and poorly financed business executives. That flushing wouldn't begin in earnest until 2007.

It wasn't that Overlook was not ready for Chinese companies; it was that Chinese companies weren't yet ready for Overlook. Our time would come, but until then, we had a saying at Overlook: "We don't invest in China because China… is China."

From our December 2003 report:

GENERAL OBSERVATIONS ON INVESTING IN CHINA

» Overlook demands that we find companies that are equally well-managed, profitable and valued as companies that we find across the rest of Asia. I do not believe that there is any justification for us to invest in China besides to earn economic returns on our investments.

» Chasing greed does not serve investors well anywhere, but particularly in China. Companies that attempt to sell a toothbrush to every Chinese citizen inevitably end in disappointment and unmet expectations.

» Patience and discipline must be exercised in pursuing investments. Despite an explosion of listed vehicles that will provide us with a rich selection of choices to gain direct and indirect exposure to China, one must remember that China's evolution from a command economy to a market economy is still in its early stage.

» Transparency in China is slowly improving. For example, I recently calculated that 35% of China's auto industry is now owned by public companies in Shanghai or Hong Kong. As this percentage rises to 60% and 70%, investors will be able to grasp with confidence the overall financial performance of the auto industry and the risks associated with specific stocks. A similar process is going on in almost every industry.

As we learned in the 1997/98 Economic Crisis, there are times when either economic or political factors expose equity investors to too much risk. Frankly, the excessive credit growth of today violates many of the early warning signs that we swore never to ignore after 1997/98. Thus, our current exposure to China is measured.

However, our ongoing research effort in China is more active than ever before.

FIVE CATEGORIES OF CHINESE
PUBLIC COMPANIES

There are five distinct categories of public companies that offer investors exposure to China in 2003. The five are listed below. In some cases, I have added a few examples to clarify each sector.

1. *State-Owned Enterprises*: These include both national, provincial and local government backed companies. SOEs are segmented by industry, geography and size. This is the biggest sector by market capitalization. There are many drawbacks to investing in SOEs. These include misaligned interests, poorly formulated growth strategies, pressure to carry out "national service," high turnover, and suspect quality of management.

2. *P-Chips*: These are public companies founded and managed by private entrepreneurs in China. Most are listed in Hong Kong and Singapore, although many eventually will be listed in Shanghai and Shenzhen. This sector will be the most dynamic, yet challenging, area for investors for many years to come. It is a major focus of Overlook's research effort.

3. *Asian Companies Moving into China*: This sector includes many Asian public companies that are expanding their core business into China. It provides us the opportunity to back managements with proven track records and quality businesses. I believe a portion of these companies will overcome the hurdles of operating as a non-Chinese entity in China.

   » Café de Coral, a great company which we have described elsewhere in this book, initially struggled in southern China with eight unprofitable stores. They were thinking of backing out. In 2002 I told Michael Chan, CdeC's chairman, "Michael, we are rich enough to keep trying in China. Don't stop trying in China." By 2005, CdeC had 31 outlets in Guangdong, all profitable, all cash flow positive, and earning higher margins than their stores in Hong Kong.

» Convenience Retail Asia, a member of the successful Li & Fung Group of Hong Kong, extended their Circle K business into Guangdong Province. It was tough going in a highly competitive market, but CR Asia grew their China business into a profitable operation of 250 stores by 2007.

» Stella Holdings manufactures and sells brand name fashion footwear worldwide. A powerful combination of a worldwide customer base, capable Taiwanese management, and low-cost China manufacturing, Stella successfully introduced overseas footwear brands to retail customers in the domestic market.

4. *Manufacturers in China Aimed at Export*: The utilization of China's low-cost labor force and infrastructure is a well-traveled path for Overlook.

» Kingboard Chemical, a champion as previously described.

» Advantech, a Taiwan-based manufacturer of customized system integration solutions to vertical markets from finance to medicine to transportation and so on. Advantech is the largest player globally and in China for an industry that many call "industrial PCs." We have held our investment in Advantech for over 13 years which generated an IRR of 25.6%. The company's Chairman, K. C. Liu, is a member of the Overlook Hall of Fame.

5. *Suppliers to China*: This group is comprised principally of commodity producers from Southeast Asia that supply China's thirst for everything from food to semiconductors to industrial raw materials. This has been a successful, low-risk way to leverage off of China's growth.

» IOI Corporation, one of Malaysia's leading palm oil producers with strong growth in sales to China. We often say China is high volume, low margin; while Malaysia is low volume, high margin. IOI succeeded in Malaysia and China through their operational excellence.

» Taiwan Semiconductor Manufacturing Company, founded in 1987 and now the largest semiconductor foundry globally, became the leading supplier to China's booming technology manufacturing sector.

FOUR PITFALLS OF INVESTING IN P-CHIPS IN 2003

There are distinct pitfalls to investing in all five of the sectors listed above. However, China's P-Chips expose investors to a unique and challenging set of pitfalls. P-Chips will provide us with great investments over the long term, so I wanted to discuss with you four specific hazards of investing with China's new entrepreneurs. I hope this section gives you a taste of the challenges we face in China.

1. *The Alpha Male Entrepreneur*: While I do not like to generalize, China's P-Chip companies are managed by the most aggressive entrepreneurs that I have ever encountered. Very typically, these entrepreneurs dominate their companies with their "I know everything" attitudes and a "growth at all costs" approach to business.

   When interviewing senior executives, we like to ask the Columbo Question, named after Peter Falk's character in the *Columbo* hit TV series that ran from the late 1960s to the early 1980s. The idea is to ask a carefully crafted question that goes right to the heart of a critical issue by playing dumb. Columbo questions are usually preceded by: "Just one more thing..." If done well, impatient executives tend to tell you what they really think.

   My favorite Columbo moment occurred during a visit to the first organic vegetable producer in China, located in Fujian province. Organic farming was at the time new to China—one might say it hadn't yet arrived—and it was experiencing rapid, if perhaps suspect, growth. After touring one of the company's farms and the main wet market of Fuzhou, we went to the company headquarters to meet with the Chairman and his COO.

After 45 minutes or so, as the meeting was winding down, I asked the Chairman my Columbo question: "Just one more thing. Umm... do you think you could grow this company by 10 to 12 percent over the next several years?" That was the minimum growth we required to buy the stock.

"What?!" he exclaimed, "What?! 10 to 12 percent?!" The Chairman sat up straight in his chair. "If I only grow at 10 to 12 percent," he said, jabbing his finger toward the COO, "I kill this guy."

We bought the stock, the company grew like a weed, and we still lost 10.7% over 2.2 years before we sold. We were happy to get out. To this day I wonder how the COO fared.

2. *The Entrepreneur's Pitfall*: There is no product in the West that is quite as ubiquitous as rice crackers in China, and Want Want China Holdings dominates the industry. Owned by a Taiwanese family, listed in Hong Kong, all of Want Want's production and sales were in China. It was a great China business, and in 2009, we were incredibly interested.

Our hesitation about Want Want was their tendency to expand into new product lines. We repeatedly advised management that they should keep their focus on the core business. It is the entrepreneur's pitfall to believe that one success is a Midas touch for anything.

A colleague and I visited one of their factories outside of Hangzhou. After touring the factory, the managers invited us to lunch to talk about the rice cracker business—but also, it turned out, to introduce us to their latest diversification: baijiu, the clear Chinese liquor.

Now, these jovial and heavy-set managers were obviously capable drinkers, and poured shots for all with insistent cheer. Sometimes in China it is best to just go along with the hospitality. My colleague, a bit of a rookie at such things, turned bright red after only a couple of shots. I said, "Let a professional take over."

For the next hour I matched these guys with the shots of baijiu. Though it was fun, that afternoon I felt especially low because Want Want, I realized, was never going to remain focused. They would continue to waste time and resources on other businesses that would never be as successful as what they already had.

3. *Weak Accounting*: I hate to complain about weak accounting, as I have benefited from a world of weak accounting for many years; but China has a disproportionate number of P-Chips that operate today with unsustainable margins and suspect business models. For example, Overlook recently purchased a large position in Vedan, a Taiwanese managed group that operates a large and sophisticated starch-based business from an integrated facility in the Mekong River Delta southeast of Ho Chi Minh City. As part of our due diligence, Overlook visited a P-Chip that operates a starch-based business in China. Not only was the Chinese company smaller, but it also lacked the sophisticated fermentation technology that provides a barrier to entry and high value-added products to the Taiwanese.

Yet, we discovered that the Chinese business is currently earning a 55% gross profit margin and the Vietnam facility earns a 25% gross profit margin. I cannot say with certainty what accounts for the difference in margin, but I can tell you I prefer to have our money invested with the Taiwanese at 25% gross profit and at 1.4 times book, as opposed to the PRC entrepreneur at 3.3 times book.

4. *Hidden Risks – Third Time Lucky*: After years of investing in Asia, I generally feel that I have seen everything; but China can still surprise.

In 1996, I was flying to Nanjing on Dragon Air to visit a company called Orient Power. I was sitting in economy class, toward the back of the plane, next to Baldwin Lee, the company's independent investment banker. After take-off, we both opened our briefcases to do some work.

It was an uneventful flight until we approached Nanjing, where thick, low-lying fog blanketed the airport. We descended through near-zero visibility, and when land finally appeared below, we were off course for the runway. The pilot pulled the plane up into an emergency climb.

As the plane circled around to make another approach, Baldwin looked at me with a nervous chuckle. We started up a conversation and began to get to know each other well. Then, for the second time, the plane came down through the fog to land, but – Whoa! – we were off course again! The engines roared for another emergency climb. We were all gripping our armrests in fear. The woman across the aisle began to sob loudly. One near crash: scary. Two on the same trip? We had already beaten the odds. Three? Not in a lifetime.

Before we could attempt a third try, the plane was diverted to the Hangzhou Air Force Base where we sat on the tarmac for over two hours before returning to Nanjing, arriving six hours late. Upon checking into the hotel, Baldwin and I took a beeline directly to the bar and we have remained fast friends ever since, often enjoying a lunch of ma po dou fu and char siu at Tsui Hang Tsuen Restaurant in New World Tower.

These experiences with alpha male entrepreneurs, baijiu lunches, and terrifying flights produced only mixed results in our work to invest in China. But China's potential remained enticing. Could we find a company in China that met the standards of our Investment Philosophy? We continued the search.

NetEase: China on Our Terms

NetEase was at that time a growing force in China's personal computer gaming industry. The company's financial track record was powerful: NetEase was a profitable, cash-generating machine with a couple of market-leading PC games. The company was founded in 1997 by a 26-year-old software engineer named William Ding. The company had listed on NASDAQ in 2000, which gave us some confidence in the financial information released to shareholders. The long bear market in China was grinding on, and NetEase shares were trading at a bargain valuation. This was worth looking into.

Shortly thereafter, NetEase hosted an investor conference at their headquarters during a dreary winter night in Hangzhou. William Ding and his management team made the presentation. I was the only foreigner, and the presentation was in Mandarin with translations specifically for me every once in a while.

So I watched, and what caught my attention was that William Ding seemed bored in front of the group, almost like he didn't want to be there, like he had better things to do than be bothered with shareholders. Who was this young man running a US$ 5.5 billion public company? Was his gift luck, or was it skill? This company was cash rich, but had never paid dividends. Was NetEase like so many other Chinese companies I had seen that didn't really care about shareholders?

Back in Hong Kong, James and I discussed NetEase and reached a decision to give William Ding the benefit of the doubt. Their main games, *Westward Journey* and *Fantasy Westward Journey*, had been around for eight and six years, respectively. They had a track record of high profitability; NetEase's core games had long-term franchise value; and the share price was low, a result of Wall Street's lack of interest in Chinese ADRs. Put together, there was just enough to convince Overlook to buy.

My initial caution about William Ding's regard for shareholders quickly dissipated. Within a month after our first purchase of shares in October

2012, NetEase announced a US$ 131 million special dividend and a share repurchase of up to US$ 100 million. Within 18 months, NetEase announced an annual dividend policy to pay approximately 25% of net income. Sales continued to grow, NetEase's market dominance increased, and the share price rose. NetEase was the real McCoy.

We reported the following to the Overlook investors in June 2013:

Interactive online games are hugely popular in China. Within the industry, MMORPGs (which stands for Massively Multiplayer Online Role-playing Games: basically, online games where large numbers of people can play simultaneously) are an especially fast-growing and highly profitable sector. MMORPGs are a big industry in China, generating over Rmb 30.8 billion (US$ 5.0 billion) in revenue in 2012, and NetEase is the largest developer and operator of MMORPGs in China.

NetEase has many qualities that Overlook looks for in our investments, namely:

1. Strong business franchise with demonstrated pricing power.

2. High financial returns and a cash rich balance sheet.

3. Attractive earnings growth prospects.

MMORPGs are incredibly lucrative if a game is a major hit. A self-developed hit game generates hundreds of millions of U.S. dollars in net income and cash flow per year. A game is considered a hit in the U.S. if it achieves over a few hundred thousand peak concurrent users (PCUs). NetEase's most popular game, *Fantasy Westward Journey*, reached 2.7 million PCUs in 2012.

At the end of 2009, NetEase had over Rmb 7 billion of cash (over US$ 1.1 billion) on its balance sheet. As we followed NetEase over 2010 and 2011, its earnings grew over 30% compounded annually so that by the middle of 2012, cash had increased to Rmb 15.4 billion (over US$ 2.5 billion).

We own NetEase for its unmatched game development capabilities and the financial returns the games generate. NetEase is the one and only game developer in China that has successfully developed hit games outside of its core franchise; to date, all of its industry peers have tried and failed. With two new self-developed games launched in late 2012 and another two expected later this year, we are confident NetEase can continue to grow earnings for its shareholders.

Overlook had finally found in NetEase a great Chinese public company and, in William Ding, an executive who could create real value for shareholders. Our investment in NetEase has since continued to grow and NetEase has become today one of the largest core holdings in our portfolio, generating for Overlook investors an annually compounded return of 44.4% for 8.4 years. William Ding, in recognition of his talent and accomplishments, is now a member of the Overlook Hall of Fame. NetEase will soon join the Decade Club.

NetEase was proof that Overlook could invest in China on our terms. We were excited, and we felt certain there were more companies like NetEase out there. We just had to find them.

The Hunt was on for Overlook in China.

The Hunt:
China: 2013–2021

To learn who rules over you, simply find out who you are not allowed to criticize.

— VOLTAIRE

AT OVERLOOK WE all consider ourselves stock pickers by profession, so we live for those rare moments in our careers when hunting for stocks to buy is like shooting fish in a barrel. And so it was that in 2013, global events were aligning to offer us one of the greatest periods of our lives as stock pickers in a market which had frustrated us for so long: China.

But before we tell that story, it will be useful to briefly explain why Overlook had turned its focus so intensely to China; and then, when we did, the unique circumstances that greeted us there.

A Bit of Background

KNOW WHEN TO WAIT

In 2006–07, a speculative bull market in China A-Shares, fueled by retail investors, sent share prices skyrocketing. At the same time, Chinese state-owned companies accelerated their listings of low-quality assets in Hong Kong with great fanfare. Such was the onslaught that on January 1, 2006, PRC Chinese companies comprised 30% of the Hang Seng Index; whereas 21 months later, on September 30, 2007, PRC Chinese companies made up 50% of the index.

During this period, officials also allowed PRC citizens to invest in Hong Kong shares for the first time ever, and the speculative stampede spilled over into the Hang Seng Index. P/E valuations on the HSI were driven to new heights, briefly exceeding the Dow Jones and S&P 500 for the first time in memory. Everybody, it seemed, had caught the China fever.

Everybody, that is, except Overlook. We wanted no part of it. The valuations were unsustainable. Anticipating that the euphoria would end in tears, Overlook decreased its allocation to Hong Kong and China to the lowest level in our history. We stayed true to our valuation discipline, increased our defensive holdings, held cash, and ignored the intoxicating allure of momentum investing. Realistic share valuation would eventually come, and Overlook was content to patiently watch and wait.

In October 2007, the bubble burst with a vengeance in both China and Hong Kong. By the end of March 2008, the CSI 300 A-Share index and the Hang Seng Index were down 72.7% and 66.0% respectively from their peaks. Investors fled – the China Dream was over. In September, Lehman Brothers filed the largest bankruptcy case in U.S. history, and the bottom fell out. Thus began the Global Financial Crisis. It was a worldwide rout.

Overlook, meanwhile, had become a buyer.

KNOW WHEN TO BUY

Recall that in the aftermath of the 1997/98 Asian Crisis, Asian economies reformed, and Asian companies reformed to create Asia's New Winners – those companies that had learned to survive and thrive. Overlook had generated average annual compounded returns of 24.9% from 2000–2007. Similarly, as share prices fell in 2008, we were given the opportunity to buy some of Asia ex-China's great companies at mouthwatering valuations. These companies comprise what we call Overlook's Class of 2008.

A record eight new investments were added to the Overlook portfolio in 2008, including Kalbe Farma, Advantech, Texwinca Holdings, Thai Beverage, and Stella Holdings. These were a second generation of Asia's Winners that we were eager to own. Simultaneously, Overlook opportunistically increased its positions in long-held investments like TSMC, Top Glove, and Chroma ATE. All of these companies had grown stronger, but their share prices had temporarily dipped in the bear market sell-off.

It was not clairvoyance that led us to buy in 2008; it was confidence in the underlying strength of Asian economies and Asian companies. Indeed, Asia avoided the worst of the global crisis, and our confidence paid off: in 2009 and 2010 Overlook achieved returns of 72.8% and 53.3%, respectively.

KNOW WHEN TO SELL

By 2012 our investments in the New Winners of the early 2000s and in the Class of 2008 had reached valuations that we could not rationally justify. P/E ratios on some of our companies climbed in excess of 30. When the whole world wants what you own and is willing to pay a price you would not pay, it is probably time to sell. We sold. Jon Bush had first labeled it "Tomorrow's Price Today."

So it was that in late 2012, Overlook had capital to deploy. Where were the best opportunities in Asia? We turned our attention to China.

The Planets Align

I mentioned that Overlook attended a NetEase presentation to investors in early 2013. Normally, in New York or Hong Kong, let alone China, one might expect that an investor presentation by a company of this caliber would lure an audience large enough to fill a hotel ballroom. But there were only 15 people in attendance and I was the only foreigner. Where was everybody?

The fact that investors just weren't interested in China at that time sparked our interest. By the end of 2012 the CSI 300 index of China share markets had fallen 63.7% from its late 2007 peak. It would finally reach bottom in March 2014, nearly seven years after the peak. With China's share markets in decline, investors, and especially international investors, had lost interest and were nowhere to be found. It felt like Overlook had the China market to itself. The planets had aligned.

A Pivotal Meeting in Shanghai

Following our investment in NetEase, Overlook began a methodical search for Chinese companies. From past experience, however, Overlook still had lingering hesitation about the ability of Chinese companies to create value for shareholders. NetEase had proven itself, but one company alone does not confirm a trend. With that in the back of my mind, I traveled to Shanghai in 2013 to meet with Huayu Auto Parts.

We were in a windowless conference room with the Huayu CFO and the Head of Investor Relations, along with a third person to whom I had not been introduced. He was seated at the far end of the conference room table, diligently taking notes, not speaking at all. I found his presence slightly annoying.

As we finished our discussion of the company's operations and financial performance, unable to find the weaknesses in Huayu that were usually uncoverable in A-Share companies, I asked the CFO, in my best New York accent: "Thank you. This has been very informative, but who is looking after the interests of Huayu's minority shareholders?"

To my surprise, the CFO said, "Mr. Lawrence, the independent directors, of course, look after your interests."

"OK, but in 28 years in Asia I have never been introduced to an independent director."

"Well," said the Head of Investor Relations, "at Huayu Auto Parts, that is not the case. Would you like to meet them?"

I subsequently met with one of the independent directors for a candid, productive and convincing meeting. Some companies in China seemed at last to be searching for ways to run public companies correctly. The meetings gave me enormous encouragement.

We invested in Huayu shares. When we bought Huayu in 2013, it was on 7 times P/E and growing E.P.S. mid-teens. It also yielded 4% with a 16% return on equity and 54% operating returns. Management and independent directors respected our input as shareholders. Huayu was a well-run public company and our investment was a success, yielding an IRR of 42.0% for Overlook's investors over two years.

By the way, that mysterious person at the other end of the conference table? He was a representative of the Communist Party. This was not an uncommon practice for public companies in China at the time, especially when a foreign investor was involved. Just as mysteriously, he never again attended any of our meetings with Huayu.

This following chart shows the CSI 300 A-Share index from January 1, 2007 to April 1, 2015.

Overlook Seizes the Opportunity

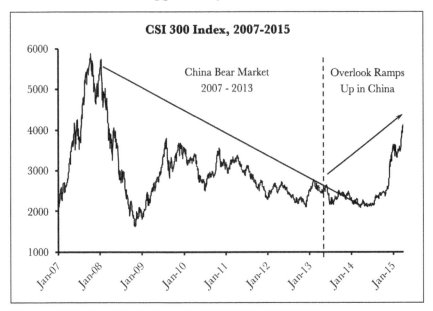

CSI 300 Index, 2007-2015

China Bear Market 2007 - 2013

Overlook Ramps Up in China

Source: Bloomberg.

A Huddle in Macau

It is said that as a stock picker there will be very few times in your career when everything is going your way. Overlook had such periods after the 97/98 Asian Crisis and the 07/08 Crisis when, with Asia's New Winners, we found great companies all across Asia. It was an incredible experience, and it taught us to recognize those rare moments of special opportunity. And now, in 2013, with our discovery of NetEase and then Huayu, we sensed that another great era of opportunity was opening for us in China.

Overlook views the universe of companies through the lens of our Investment Philosophy, and Chinese companies were finally moving into that selective field. After seven years of declining share prices in China, we were finding companies that had the size and sophistication to handle China's enormous potential. Just a few years earlier we had said, "We don't invest in China because China is China." Now it seemed we would be able to invest in China on our own terms.

At the 2013 annual offsite meeting of the Overlook Investment Team in Macau, we had one item on the agenda: China. Everybody prepared for the meeting by bringing a list of Chinese companies to pursue. I started the discussion with 10 companies, then James came up with the next 10, then the Investment Team came up with another 20! It was electrifying. If there is one thing Overlook does well, it is the Hunt – and the Hunt was now on for companies in China. Enthusiasm among the Investment Team that night at the Blackjack tables was bubbling over. We were on the doorstep of one of the greatest periods of stock picking of our career.

QFII? Small Fee

There was, however, one obstacle to Overlook's access into China: since 2002, PRC regulations restricted foreign investment in China's A-Share markets to those licensed under the Qualified Foreign Institutional Investor program (QFII, pronounced "Q-Fee"). Overlook applied for an initial QFII license to invest US\$ 200 million but received an allocation of only US\$ 100 million. Most of the QFII allocation had been granted to the usual suspects: the big-name investment management companies in New York, Tokyo, and London with big public relations departments. Who was Overlook?

In order to invest in the great companies Overlook was finding, we needed QFII capacity; and those who had it, as it turned out, didn't want it. The clients of the big international firms were exhausted by seven years of declining prices in China A-Shares, and Mike Lonergan, Overlook's CEO and CFO, managed to rent their QFII capacity for a small annual fee. They thought we were crazy, but this is what a seven-year bear market does to investors.

A Stock Picker's Paradise

A brief bull market in China A-Shares in late 2014 and early 2015 momentarily slowed our pace, but then A-Shares corrected and Overlook moved right back in. The dice were rolling our way. How fast could we move? It was a stock picker's paradise, something we encounter so rarely in our careers. The opportunities kept coming and we kept buying.

Despite this significant change in Overlook's asset allocation, we kept quiet about our work in China, even to Overlook's investors. Amongst international investors we had the market nearly to ourselves and we were scared to let anybody know about the bonanza we had found.

Overlook's China activity is reflected in the growing allocation of our portfolio to China, as shown in the following table.

Overlook Portfolio Allocation to China

Year	Allocation to China	AUM of Overlook
2010	6.6%	US$ 1.79 bn
2011	9.7%	US$ 1.92 bn
2012	18.1%	US$ 2.73 bn
2013	30.9%	US$ 3.36 bn
2014	45.6%	US$ 3.63 bn
2015	56.5%	US$ 3.74 bn
2020	55.3%	US$ 7.10 bn

The Thrill of the Hunt

For Overlook in China, the opportunities kept coming and we kept buying.

From 2013 to 2015 Overlook invested in some of China's greatest companies: domestic leaders, international powerhouses, irreplaceable infrastructure assets, and online giants. These were China's future blue chips and they were available to Overlook at bargain valuations.

The pace of our investment was intense. By the end of 2015, Overlook had invested US$ 2.11 billion in China. And by the end of 2017, the gains alone on our China investments exceeded US$ 1.43 billion.

In our March 2016 report to investors, we had the following to say:

> Overlook's history will eventually show that the 2013–2015 rotation into China was one of the most insightful allocation shifts in our 25-year existence. In Q2 and Q3 2014, tiny Overlook was probably the largest foreign buyer of A-Shares in the world. This accomplishment was the result of total team effort at Overlook.

The thrill of picking stocks in China can only be described in the opportunities we were finding. Four examples are described below.

CHINA YANGTZE POWER COMPANY: PREDICTABLE CASH FLOW

One of the companies we discussed during our meeting in Macau was China Yangtze Power Company (CYPC), owner of the famous Three Gorges hydroelectric dam on the Yangtze River.

From our December 2014 report:

> CYPC is the largest supplier of renewable energy in China, as well as one of the largest hydroelectric generators in the world. Overlook considers the Three Gorges Dam as one of the rare 100-year assets in Asia. More importantly, Overlook believes CYPC is one of the highest quality and most reliable generators of free cash flow in China, if not Asia. And we don't say this lightly.

LOW-COST GENERATOR OF ELECTRICITY IN CHINA

The ideal moat for a business is to be the low-cost provider of an identifiably superior product. In the case of CYPC, it is the lowest cost provider of electricity in China. And just as importantly, the principal raw material (water) is essentially free, so the cost of producing electricity from the Three Gorges Dam is largely fixed and stable. This gives us confidence that CYPC is surrounded by a deep moat and will sell all of its electricity at a profit for decades to come.

A CASH MACHINE

Overlook's analysis of public companies focuses on their cash flow and free cash flow. At the core of CYPC's strength is its ability to generate approximately 87% cash gross profit margins (gross profit plus depreciation divided by sales) and 83% EBITDA margins. Maintenance capex has averaged less than 5% of gross cash flow, leaving 95% of cash flow as free cash flow to be allocated between the retention by the company for future growth, repayment of debt, and payment of dividends to shareholders. I haven't seen such high cash gross margins combined with low maintenance capex ratios many times in my career.

Photo by Stephen Wilkes.

MIDEA: THE WINNER FROM 30 YEARS OF CONSOLIDATION

Overlook is always looking for companies that have survived the consolidation phase of their industries. You may recall from an earlier chapter that back in the mid-1990s, when Overlook was chasing rainbows in China, we visited a company called Wo Kee Hong, a manufacturer of air conditioners in southern China that turned out to be one of hundreds of companies all competing in the same nascent market.

Twenty years later there were only three significant air conditioning manufacturers left standing in China. Overlook invested in one of them, an excellent company called Midea, which in that short period had become one of the largest appliance manufacturers in the world.

Surviving the intense competition of industry consolidation requires discipline and focus, and by the time we invested in Midea in 2014, the effects were apparent in the company's rising margins:

	2010	2014
Gross Profit	18.2%	25.4%
Operating Profit	5.3%	9.1%
Net Margin	1.2%	7.6%
Return on Equity	13.3%	29.7%

Midea became not just a profitable company, but a well-run public company with low debt, high cash flow, clear paths to continued growth in domestic and global markets, and an attractive valuation made even better by shareholder dividends. Upon these strengths, our investment in Midea achieved an IRR of 43.2% over two years.

Having survived industry consolidation to rise as a leader in China, Midea has also risen to industry leadership in the world and exemplifies our saying: Big in Asia, Big in the World.

SIA: AN IRREPLACEABLE INFRASTRUCTURE ASSET

Shanghai International Airport is the largest airport in Shanghai and the predominant gateway for international travel in East China. The airport has four runways, two terminals and two satellite terminals, handles over 75 million passengers per year, and is the largest cargo airport in Asia.

But can an airport be considered a growth business? The facts tell the story. In 2015, the first full year of Overlook's investment in SIA, passenger throughput rose 16.2% and international travelers rose 17.9%, while regional GDP only increased 5.6%. For the future, we note that in 2014 PRC aviation passengers totaled 61% of China's total population. In the same year, U.S. and Japanese aviation passengers totaled 267% and 208% of their respective populations.

SIA actually offers *two* paths of growth:

1. *Infrastructure asset*: SIA generates revenue from airlines and cargo handlers for landing rights and gate access, baggage handling, hangar space, storage and office space, etc. It is a large and complex business as well as a profitable growth business.

2. *Retail real estate asset*: SIA has 300,000 square feet of retail space in the terminals. The retail space is occupied by high-quality tenants with virtually guaranteed foot traffic and generates some of the highest sales per square foot in the retail industry. SIA's retail leases call for a minimum rent plus a percentage of sales: half of SIA's revenues are from retail leases, so as sales grow, lease revenues grow. To that end, note that consumer spending in China doubled between 2010 and 2015 at a compounded annual growth rate of 14.9%. For comparison, U.S. consumer sales in the same period grew by a CAGR of 3.8%.

Overlook purchased shares in SIA in 2014 at an unlevered cap rate of 14% plus a dividend yield, an unbeatable price for an irreplaceable infrastructure asset with world-class retail real estate. The investment returned an IRR of 54.1% over 5.4 years to our investors.

SHANDONG WEIGAO: A DOMESTIC LEADER FOR THE LONG TERM

Shandong Weigao (Weigao) is the largest medical consumables company in China, with leading market shares in single-use medical consumables such as syringes, infusion sets, etc. It is thus a valuable recurring revenue business with no correlation to macroeconomic slowdown.

At the time of our investment in Weigao, healthcare spend per capita in China had been growing at 16% CAGR in the previous ten years, but at US$ 510 per capita, this was still significantly below that of OECD countries. An aging population, better insurance coverage, and improvement of medical standards will, according to a report published by the China National Health Development Research Centre, continue to drive healthcare spending to grow at 8.5% p.a. until 2035.

One trait we always look for in companies is the ability to maintain revenue growth without sacrificing margins. Weigao's revenue growth compounded by 24.5% annually from 2004 through 2019. And yet Weigao, with a strong record of product innovation and an ability to introduce higher-margin products, was actually able to increase gross margins from 40.0% to 62.8% over the same period – an impressive feat.

In the mid-2000s Weigao was a hugely popular growth stock, but then was largely forgotten by the investment community. This lack of attention and the correspondingly low share price were undeserved. Weigao is a market-leading company with growth, high margins, low debt, market leadership, and proven management, selling at a low valuation. That's an Overlook company. In the five years that we have owned Weigao shares, the investment has achieved an IRR of 33.7%. We believe Weigao may well be a long-term compounder in the Overlook portfolio.

Bifurcation in China's A-Shares

Fundamental to our allocation of capital to China was our anticipation of a bifurcation of stock market performance. The separation between the limited number of high-quality companies that met Overlook's investment requirements, and those that did not – including companies that were overly indebted and/or unable or unwilling to manage a public company for the benefit of all shareholders – would drive Overlook's returns in its China A-Share holdings.

By mid-2015, bifurcation was indeed beginning to occur and blue chips were now beginning to emerge. The following chart graphically depicts the bifurcation of the Chinese companies into "the best and the rest," and the comparative performance of Overlook's investments in the "best."

A-Share Performance Since Overlook's First Purchase

Source: Bloomberg, Overlook.

A Remarkable Journey

Overlook's China journey has spanned the full chronology of China's historic and dramatic rise. It started back in 1986 when Dennis Ting told me that his relatives in southern China were doing some simple assembly work for his company, Kader Industries. Then we chased rainbows in the early 1990s by trying to sell a toothbrush to every person in China. Then came Kingboard, a Hong Kong company that had figured out how to do business in China. And then, nearly 30 years after meeting with Dennis Ting, Overlook was investing in Chinese companies that had become some of the largest companies in the world:

- World's top five computer game creator

- World's largest white goods manufacturer

- World's largest hydroelectric generator

- World's second-largest auto glass manufacturer

- China's largest auto part manufacturer

- China's second-largest search engine

- China's second-largest international airport

For all of the excitement and success of Overlook's work in China in these recent years, Overlook remains a value investor throughout all of Asia. Today our portfolio is allocated roughly 55% to Greater China and 45% to the rest of Asia, for it is not just China that has grown and matured, it is all of Asia. And as all of Asia has risen, so has the world changed.

PART FOUR

The Voices of Overlook

Overlook is comprised of a small, focused team, incentivized by performance-based, long-term compensation. Our executives succeed only after Overlook succeeds.

— RICHARD H. LAWRENCE, Jr.

W E HAVE SAID many times in this book that Overlook's Investment Philosophy and Business Practices create outperformance above an index and nearly guarantee the delivery of that outperformance to investors. It is also true that the very best Investment Philosophy and Business Practices still need to be executed.

As I think about Overlook's execution of The Model, several factors are essential.

First, Hong Kong's magic starts with the Hong Kong people. They are fluent in business from birth, possess an amazing ability to reinvent themselves at times of change, are hard-working, and have a genetic sense of the global flows of money, capital and talent. These advantages are situated in perhaps the most physically dramatic city in the world. While more than half of Overlook's staff comes from overseas, all of us were drawn to Hong Kong because we also share many of these traits. It would be nearly impossible to assemble Overlook's team in New York, London, or Shanghai.

Second, my colleagues have been huge contributors to Overlook's success. We have discussed several times in this book that while I may get credit for piecing together the core components of The Overlook Model, all of my colleagues deserve enormous credit for the execution of The Model. Overlook is not just one employee making all the calls. It is a team – dare I say, a family. There are not enough pages in this book to sufficiently honor the employees, and for this I apologize.

In this part of the book, we are switching tacks. I asked James, Leonie and William to each pick a subject of their choosing and contribute a chapter:

- "The Art of Selling Equities," contributed by James Squire.

- "Lunch with Overlook: An Interview with Jeffrey Lu Minfang," CEO of China Mengniu Dairy Co., Ltd., contributed by Leonie Foong.

- An interview with members of the Overlook Board of Advisors titled "Hong Kong, Our Home," moderated by William Leung.

- "ESG: The Climate Divergence," contributed by Richard H. Lawrence, Jr.

The Art of Selling Equities

Contributed by James Squire

The best way to manage risk is to understand what you are investing in.

— OLD WALL STREET SAYING

Biography of James Squire

In the 1990s in Hong Kong, James was often the only other foreigner at the earnings announcements of many of my favorite companies and his presence frankly pissed me off. This was my territory. We would subtly acknowledge each other's existence without talking. That is when I learned James is nearly as competitive as me.

Then we were introduced to each other and we realized each of us would be stronger working together. We had different backgrounds and education but shared a natural commitment to the fundamental principles that now comprise The Overlook Model.

I knew James was right for Overlook on a taxi ride into Seoul from Incheon Airport. For over an hour, we traded stories of Korean companies that we had both owned in the early 1990s. These included: Baik Yang, an underwear manufacturer; Suheung, gelatin capsule manufacturer; Korea Explosives, a property play; Heung-A Shipping, a bankrupt shipping company that traded on the Rehabilitation Board; and a Korean hair dye company for men, the name of which we have both forgotten, but both owned. This is just the start of the names we laughed about. It was a comedy of mistakes and frustrations.

It has been my great privilege to work alongside James, Overlook's Chief Investment Officer, these past 14 years. When I asked my Partners to write a chapter, it was natural that James would discuss the Art of Selling Equities. James is the best seller of securities I have ever witnessed. This is a chapter loaded with insights and lessons.

The Art of Selling Equities

MOST INVESTORS CONCUR that selling is the hard part of investing. There is always a clear reason to buy: because the shares appear cheap. The hard part starts once an investment has gone up. Questions as to why, when, and how one sells the position arise upon success. If the investment loses money, these questions come earlier and are no easier.

In our September 2013 quarterly report, Richard wrote about The Art of Selling Equities. In life, truths, ethics, and values remain fundamentally unchanged; but one's understanding of these qualities and insights may evolve with experience and standing in a changing world.

With that in mind, here we provide an updated commentary on selling equities: the five reasons to sell become six, and we more deeply explore our thoughts related to Tomorrow's Price Today.

Early Experience

My early history of managing money in Asia is littered with examples of selling good investments too early. A name that left me with a scar is Johnson Electric. It is a blue-chip Hong Kong manufacturer making micro motors. During my stint in Japan earlier in the 1990s I had come to know its peer, Mabuchi Motors. Johnson Electric had double the growth and traded on half the valuation. We invested in June 1996 at HK$ 4.8 and then sold three years later at HK$ 21, feeling chuffed. The stock continued to rally strongly before finally peaking in June 2000 at over HK$ 50.

Perhaps my most shameful multiple mistakes around a single name relate to Techtronic Industries, another Hong Kong manufacturer. It was a micro-cap when we invested in it in mid-1999 at under HK$ 0.5. I remember its founder, Horst Pudwill, coming into our office and excitedly showing me the multiple uses of their new Stanley knife before managing to cut himself with its blade. We sold it in June 2002 at HK$ 2.60 for a nice gain. Inexplicably, we failed to continue to follow it. When an opportunity to reinvest in it at HK$ 5.4 emerged in early 2010 after a stumble, we were unprepared, swung and missed. The market later presented another buying opportunity in 2016, with the same failed outcome. Today, the stock is happily sitting at HK$ 139 – inexcusable! I guess with some stocks one just has a mental block. Clearly, this is both irrational and a shame.

We made great money in both Johnson Electric and Techtronic Industries, but left far greater amounts on the table. My excuse? We were unable to monitor their corporate developments closely enough because our portfolio was too diverse; and our surprise at the size of the gains encouraged our timidity at a time when bravery and understanding would have served us well. I did not fully comprehend the real power of long-term investing until I took refuge under Overlook's umbrella. Since then we have become a little better at holding on to our winners and letting go of the less capable investments.

A final confession – I have also found myself selling positions too late. Little is as depressing as selling a stock knowing it has passed its sell-by date. This increases the likelihood of treating it as gum on one's shoe and then getting rid of it at any price, only to find the stock rebounding having just finished selling. To set about avoiding such outcomes, investors need to be early both in buying and selling.

The best way to ensure a correct exit is to think about an investment's duration.

Understanding the Investment: Duration

Two of our favorite sayings at Overlook are: "You don't really know a stock until you own it," and "The best way to manage risk is by understanding what you are investing in."

Before we initiate any new position, we write an investment thesis stating its opportunities and risks. In doing so, the investment is categorized, in Overlook terminology, into one of the following groups:

- Tier 1, 2, 3

- Superior Cyclicals

- Defensives

- Financials

For practitioners of this system, a stock's categorization provides a clear sense of its duration. In effect, the referencing provides a mental map with time and returns as the axis.

A comment about the "investment pace" at Overlook needs to be made.

Our mantra is: "400/40/4." This refers to analysts meeting 400 companies a year, to make 40 significant pieces of research a year, for the investment committee to make four to five investments a year. As Overlook typically owns 20 to 24 stocks, the pace assumes the portfolio will be turned over approximately every four years, as indeed has been the case. Naturally, this influences duration and focuses our efforts on investing for the long term.

Six Reasons to Sell

There are six main reasons for fund managers to sell their holdings. We have listed them below in order of least frequent first, which flows broadly from simple to more complex explanations.

1. Acquisitions

2. Mistakes

3. More ideas than space in the portfolio

4. Rebalancing

5. Changing Investment Thesis

6. Tomorrow's Price Today

We will now look at each of these more closely.

1. ACQUISITIONS

Corporate activity in Asia tends to be less frenetic than in the Western markets. Ownership structures, security laws, legal recourse, and the way of doing business all combine to make Asia's mergers and acquisitions transactions relatively infrequent. When and where they do occur, minority shareholders are poorly protected. Consequently, Overlook avoids names linked to the potential for such activity.

Since 2007, on only five occasions has Overlook been forced to sell a name through corporate activity. Two of these names were Chinese listed ADRs: Qihoo and Giant Interactive. Both have since relisted on the A-Share markets, but in markedly different forms from the entities we had previously owned. Two stocks, Unisteel and ARA, were purchased by private equity sponsored deals, leaving only Phoenixtec Power, listed in Taiwan, as a bona fide acquisition by a corporate.

2. MISTAKES

Mistakes, in our experience, are more usually about people than businesses. Recognizing one has misjudged a company's management is not easy. The desire to give management the benefit of the doubt is strong. We constantly remind ourselves that we cannot do a good deal with a bad person, yet still we make mistakes. This is both infuriating and belittling. Here are two examples of mistakes in which good businesses were neutered by management.

Daekyo is a leading education company listed in South Korea. It also had a stake in Shinhan Bank worth almost as much as its market valuation. We begged the founder in 2007 to sell its non-core asset and to invest in online education to complement its offline operations. Our advice was ignored and we sold, barely breaking even. The Global Financial Crises rolled through, the bank's financial holding halved, and online education took off. Its price today remains below where it was when we sold.

Qunxing Paper, listed in Hong Kong, was owned by a Chinese entrepreneur, Dr. Zhu. The decorative paper operations generated fabulous returns and abundant free cash flows. It was Dr. Zhu's other interests, wind farms, which became the issue. They had inferior economics and he wished to inject these assets into our listed company. Fortunately, Overlook's 4.8% stake was sufficient to block the transaction at the EGM. Then, by some miracle, a small rights issue provided sufficient liquidity for Overlook to exit the investment at a profit. And what of the company and Dr. Zhu? The stock has been suspended for a number of years. As for the good doctor, it was our discovery that he had purchased the doctorate that initially alerted us to concerns about his integrity.

3. MORE IDEAS THAN SPACE IN THE PORTFOLIO

The hypothetical "red-headed stepchild" analogy comes to mind in thinking about times when the investment team has more good ideas than we have space for in the fund. Of course, we hold dear all of our investments. We would like to say we love them equally, but that cannot be the case since they are sized differently. When a clearly superior proposition is discovered, a weaker holding is always found and makes way for our new love.

How does one know a superior investment has been found? The simplest way is to compare the new idea's investment characteristics to that of the existing portfolio. A level deeper is to compare it with its relevant Overlook tier. Finally, consideration will be given as to the portfolio utility (in plain English: diversification benefits) it brings.

It is fair to say that little brings greater satisfaction to the investment committee at Overlook than when we realize we can upgrade the portfolio through a stock forcing its way in. We have yet to shed tears for any outgoing name.

4. REBALANCING

There are various aspects to consider when discussing rebalancing. At Overlook, we start with the premise that we are more likely to make money when we are sitting on our hands rather than trading feverishly, much to the annoyance of our brokers. Unlike many fund managers, trading around positions is a minor part of what we do. Rather, it is the importance of understanding each investment's duration – through "tiering" – that helps to construct an appropriate trading plan.

Rebalancing is best understood and has meaningful investment impact when discussing large – usually top five – portfolio positions. These tend to be outsized winners. They have grown their way to the top. We are cautious about reducing our winners as we recognize investment returns are typically derived from relatively few stocks.

Rebalancing can be a simple acknowledgement that the future is uncertain. Qihoo in 2013/14 is one such example, where we top sliced on a few occasions. The mid-year results unexpectedly disappointed, which led to price weakness. These were followed by a somewhat disappointing tender offer to take the company private. The delisting was convoluted and not completed until mid-2016. During the interim, the stock traded 25% lower from where we had sold some two years earlier.

Rebalancing is often a cathartic experience. Overlook found this to be the case with CP All over 2012/13. Rebalancing allows one to make the initial decision to sell. It makes a difficult decision easy by releasing the emotional blockage. Rebalancing is effectively saying, "We are not selling, we are rebalancing. If the stock goes down, we can buy back."

An aspect that is often overlooked is that rebalancing encourages investors to hold on to positions longer. The process of appropriately sizing permits holding the stock longer, enabling larger gains over longer periods. Our investment in TSMC, held for 20 years and counting, is a good example of this. We have taken money off the table and have added back, but if not for rebalancing, we probably would have sold our entire position. Failing to rebalance would have initially delivered higher profits to the Overlook investors, but over the long term, substantially smaller profits as the stock has risen to heights we never anticipated.

5. CHANGING INVESTMENT THESIS

Before every investment is made, the stock lead on the idea writes an Investment Thesis paper. The document is just one page and presents a clear case for the investment. The focus is secular rather than cyclical and, thus, broad rather than narrow. The idea is to keep us honest. If we are correct, wonderful. But if the share rallies for reasons that we had not anticipated, it is just that lady luck has been kind to us. We do not change the narrative to align with the outcome.

Drifting from the thesis is a reason to sell. Thesis drift largely occurs from one of three sources:

1. *A low probability event taking place*: Investment theses under the section "Key Risks" will include a description of possible long-tail risks that have a low probability of occurrence. The investment decision might be good, but if the event is triggered, the outcome becomes bad, or rather, unlucky. We trip over such situations from time to time. A recent example is Beijing Shanghai High Speed Railway in early 2020, where the steady, irreplaceable asset's defensive operations were eviscerated by the outbreak of COVID. Fortunately, we had already sold.

2. *A change in strategy*: Corporates are living entities and so change through time. These changes are not always for the better, as we have discovered to our woes. Our attempts to remain close with management are targeted to ensure that we are not taken by surprise by the launch of a new business arm, or alike. Our clear preference is for simple, focused businesses, so it was a great disappointment when Kingboard Chemical Holdings in 2010 decided to diversify into properties at the listed level rather than keeping these interests private. Within a year we had sold out, ending a decade of wonderful partnership with Kingboard.

3. *A poor corporate transaction*: Little shocks us as greatly as when we hear one of our holdings has overpaid, overdiversified, or made a questionable interparty related transaction. Fear, sweat and anger are the aftereffects of the news. CP All's acquisition of Siam Makro in April 2013 is seared in my memory as one such example. Here, a top dollar valuation was paid for a business that CP Group had been forced to sell during the Asian Crisis. It took the company from a net cash position to net debt/EBITDA of 4.5x! Furthermore, it was Overlook's largest holding at the time and had previously graduated from Overlook's Modern Finance Technology class.

The lesson is that surprises arise despite the best laid plans. Reacting appropriately is critical. More often than not, I have found it right to follow my late mother's advice: "A stitch in time saves nine."

6. TOMORROW'S PRICE TODAY

We define Tomorrow's Price Today as being offered a price which is substantially above what one feels is fair value for the item. There may be good reasons not to sell – such as the item is irreplaceable, or it has great sentimental value. With regards to equities, we view Tomorrow's Price as when the market is discounting too far into the future: at least two years, but not unusually three years or more.

When one is getting tomorrow's price today, greed frequently trumps reason, preventing the would-be seller from transacting. The desire to hold on for more subdues rational thought. The price that was previously acceptable is no longer. In my experience, residential property vendors best exhibit this kind of irrational seller behavior.

There are times when a market can be speculatively and wildly overvalued. Such examples include Wall Street in 1929, 2000 and 2008; or China in 2007 and 2015. Such occasions generally end in brutal and painful crashes, leaving psychological investment scars. However, exiting while the party is in full swing is hard, and it is dangerous to bet against bull markets. The famous economist Lord Keynes noted, "Markets can remain irrational longer than you can remain solvent." Moreover, at Overlook we joke internally that we have predicted eight of the last two market crashes.

Overlook sees underperforming the later stages of a bull market as a badge of honor. At such times, the wrong people are making quick money. Real money, we believe, is made slowly. The most speculative stocks do well at peaks. Since we take great care and pride in not overpaying, it is almost impossible for us to outperform at such times. This helps to explain the Overlook investors' underperformance in 2007 when we had sold out of China and the market was raging. However, we were more than able to recover the underperformance in the following years as Chinese shares crashed in 2008. A similar set of circumstances and outcomes occurred from 1998 to 2001.

Duration and Selling

Earlier in this chapter, under "Understanding the Investment: Duration," we touched upon the importance of categorization. We will now discuss the mental models we use for the Tier 3, Superior Cyclicals, and Tier 1 categories, since they represent the basic spectrum of how we approach selling.

TIER 3

Tier 3 businesses are what Warren Buffett would describe as "cigar butts." These businesses are our least favored type of investment and rarely account for more than 6% of the book (one to two positions). Our approach here is to buy them very cheaply and expect to sell them cheaply with the knowledge that time is working against the investment. We never hold such positions for more than 36 months. If money is made quickly, the IRR is realized and we move on.

Tier 3 Business – Time Works Against You

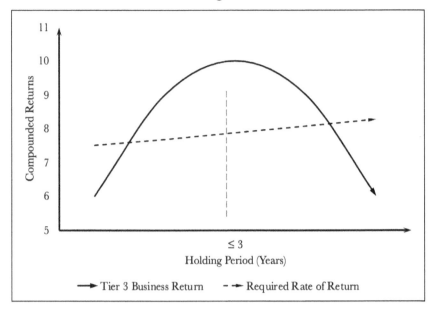

SUPERIOR CYCLICALS

Superior Cyclicals are those companies that generate high operating returns and require limited fixed asset and working capital investment, but are cyclical in nature. Consequently, this group tends to carry lower multiples than stocks with similar investment returns that are more stable. The earnings volatility provides the opportunity, but investors need to avoid buying at the wrong part of the cycle. 10–25% of the book (three to six positions) is invested in such names.

For Superior Cyclicals, the length of the holding period is largely business cycle dependent. The possibility of holding the names through multiple cycles exists, but it is more likely that the position is sold with the hope of revisiting the name at the next business downturn.

Superior Cyclical – Earnings Power Critical

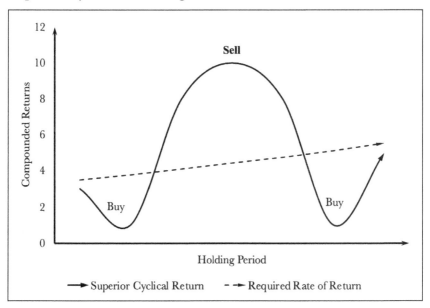

The classic Overlook Superior Cyclical example is Top Glove, the world's top manufacturer of latex rubber gloves, listed in Malaysia. The company is run by the very capable Tan Sri Dato' Lee Shin-cheng, and Malaysia has a competitive advantage in sourcing latex due its extensive rubber plantations. Overlook took an outsized position in 2004. We understood that rubber prices and the operating margins moved in opposite directions and Top Glove made a flat fee (roll margin) per piece. Thus, when demand was high but rubber prices were low, windfall profits were made. Such circumstances arose in 2010; so, when the market discounted the current margins into perpetuity, we took advantage and sold, having made three and a half times our initial cost.

ASM Pacific, another Superior Cyclical, has the accolade of being sold and repurchased four times – more than any other stock in Overlook's history – generating a combined IRR of 117.9%. It makes back-end testing equipment that is tied closely to the semiconductor industry. Cutting to the chase, we have conviction around the earnings power – the earnings per share the company can generate – of ASM's operations. This enables us to value the business in a downturn when the market is fearful. Moreover, it anchors us in the upturn when brokers, often new to the name, revise up their fair value multiples based on peak earnings.

TIER 1

Tier ɪ businesses are a very different investment proposition since time works for investors. Characteristically, they enjoy exceptionally high returns; have low capital intensity, strong pricing power, and defensible moats; and are cash generative. One needs to be wary of selling such gems, since their duration is infinity. The catch is that few companies are ranked Tier ɪ. We seek Tier ɪ to occupy as large a portion of the book as possible.

Tier 1 Business – Time Works For You

Tier ɪ businesses are the most likely candidates for rebalancing. When the stock price runs ahead of earnings, it may be advisable to trim the position, then wait for earnings to grow and chew through the overvaluation. Selling out with the idea of repurchasing rarely happens, as the market recognizes the value and is not prepared to offer the stock at a discount. Therefore, the best one can hope for is to buy these great businesses at fair value and sit with them, allowing for the magic of compounding. Tier 1 businesses Overlook has written about over the years include Unilever Indonesia, TSMC and NetEase, to name a few.

A caveat to remember is that companies can transition between tiers, more often down than up. This is often the reason behind exiting Tier 1 names. Recognizing the change is often the reason to sell. The reasons behind the change are manifold but include a quantum slowdown in growth, changing business landscape, a morphing investment story and technological obsolescence.

Summary

The selling of an investment is driven by our understanding of the investment. Investments have different durations that derive from the risks associated with them. Knowing whether time is working for or against an investment is a crucial first step. With insights, an appropriate exit strategy can be constructed. Overlook's tiering system guides as to the likely manner of the sale. Accordingly, we have made this a component of The Overlook Model.

We should not give the impression that the approach is infallible. We believe it nudges the odds in our favor. As much as possible, we avoid looking back at what was left on the table. We are aware that one cannot catch the top of stocks just as one cannot catch the trough. Supposedly, Lord Rothschild, on being asked how he became so wealthy, replied: "By leaving the last 10% on the table."

Lunch with Overlook:
An Interview with Jeffrey Lu Minfang

Contributed by Leonie Foong

If you don't stay with your winners, you are not going to be able to pay for the losers.

— JACK D. SCHWAGER,
Market Wizards

Biography of Leonie Foong

Leonie is a Partner at Overlook Investments and a member of the Investment Committee. She has a wonderful mix of characteristics that are perfectly suited to the fund management business. Whereas my competitiveness hides in plain sight, Leonie brings a smile, politeness, and caring to all facets of Overlook that often obscures her drive and focus. Corporate executives underestimate Leonie at their peril. They should know that she is incredibly disciplined and has a growth mindset, a tireless work ethic, an encyclopedic memory and an unwavering commitment to The Overlook Model. Her judgment and frank opinions have made her a good sounding board within Overlook and to external corporate executives. All of us agree that it was a fine day when Leonie agreed to join us.

When I asked Leonie what she wanted to write about, her version of "Lunch with the *FT*" was a topic perfectly chosen and beautifully written.

"When you have growth, you have time to fix issues."

I N AN UNPRECEDENTED year marked by Covid-19 disruptions and inflationary pressures on raw milk supply, Jeffrey Lu Minfang, CEO of China Mengniu Dairy Co., Ltd., who is a member of the Overlook Hall of Fame, has led the company to a quick recovery and built strong foundations for long-term growth ahead. Over curry chicken and panna cotta, Jeffrey talks to me about leadership, East-West differences, and how he is driving long-term sustainable growth.

I am putting the finishing touches on my curry chicken and decorating my panna cotta with a swirl of jujube topping. Given quarantine restrictions, my lunch with Mengniu's CEO is virtual. I have scheduled a time and date with his assistant but have not been told which venue or what food he will be eating. Not knowing what to expect, I think it will be fitting for me to eat what I invest in: curry chicken and panna cotta made with Mengniu's products.

Shortly after 12:00 noon, Jeffrey appears on Zoom. He is dialing in from his office in Beijing. He is a football fan. There are two framed soccer jerseys on the wall behind him. One is a distinctive blue and white striped No. 10 Argentina shirt signed by Messi himself. Jeffrey has been a superstar and team player at Mengniu, not unlike Messi on the football field.

I first met Jeffrey in March 2016 at a breakfast meeting with a colleague. At that time he was the CEO of Yashili, an infant formula company in which Mengniu has a 51.4% stake. We had just become shareholders of Mengniu. I was impressed by Jeffrey's ability to hone in on the key issues that Yashili was facing and articulate a clear strategy for fixing them. Mengniu's board must have felt the same way. Six months later, facing underperformance in Mengniu's core franchise and a languishing share price, Jeffrey was appointed to take over as CEO of the whole company.

Jeffrey aimed high and set a target to grow revenues by 20% p.a., double the growth rate that Mengniu had delivered in the previous three years. Those targets were considered ambitious and many were skeptical. However, since then Jeffrey has delivered top line growth and margin improvements that would be the envy of any consumer staple company.

When I ask him to reflect on how this turnaround was achieved, he leaves me in no doubt. "Team alignment," he responds immediately.

"The biggest gain [from the previous regime] is we have a very strong leadership team that is in alignment. Very united teams at leadership level and also at the business unit level. We have very clear alignment from the top to the operational level. We are talking about the same thing. That is the biggest gain."

This had not been the case before at Mengniu. "People might have aligned views during a meeting, but when they walk out, they would do different things."

"How do you create alignment?" I ask, trying to tease out actionable ideas as opposed to just management catchphrases.

"We started with the strategic plan that I developed together with my team. We got buy-in from everyone on what we should do," he explains. He pauses to emphasize his next point. "Then, most importantly, is who you choose to be on the executive team. I changed 11 out of the 12 executive members within the first six months." He explains, "It is an important signal to the entire organization as to who we think are the right leaders for the organization. When everybody agrees on who are the right leaders, it is much easier to communicate from top to bottom."

I nodded in agreement. Jeffrey has put a lot of thought into how to create an aligned team. He adds, "When you have a strategy, you *must* have the team mindset to act as truly one team. We make decisions together, we take responsibility together, but at the same time, we each have our own responsibility and we deliver on what we are supposed to do."

It occurs to me that this sounds incredibly similar to what Richard always says when we make investment decisions at Overlook. We decide as a team: if something goes wrong, we own the problem as a team; no finger pointing.

Where did Jeffrey's management philosophy come from? As he shares the arc of his career, it dawns on me he has actually had a pitch-side view of evolving management practices in China over the past three decades. Given Mengniu itself has both Danone and COFCO (a Chinese SOE) as major shareholders, I deliberately ask a loaded question: "Do you see yourself as a bridge of East and West?"

He deftly reframes the question by giving me a history of how Western and Chinese companies operating in China have evolved over time. "There is a huge difference. The time scale is even more interesting," he begins.

Unknown to most is that Jeffrey's first job after graduating from college was at a state-owned pharmaceutical company in a R&D role. His dream was to be a scientist and his degree was in genetics and biochemistry. Jeffrey recalled only working two or three hours each day at the state-owned company; things were slow and people were not motivated. He was attracted to the entrepreneurial environment at the multi-national companies (MNCs) in those days.

"The first generation of leaders at the MNCs, when they came into China, they brought a lot, in terms of sales, marketing, leadership, and business management practices that were lacking in China. They moved fast, made decisions quickly and you could feel the high energy level."

He moved to GE Medical in China, which he credits as being a "good training ground in leadership and sales," before spending nine years at Johnson & Johnson, then moving to Danone where he stayed for 11 years and oversaw the success of its baby nutrition business in China. He clearly favored Western companies and management practices for much of his career, and he endorses the choice his son has made to double major in psychology and business at the Stern School of Business in New York. These days, though, he finds the MNCs have evolved from being entrepreneurial to being relatively slow-moving organizations.

"At that time, the U.S. and Europe were very much advanced in terms of consumer trends, in innovation. Today, China is moving very fast. If you just apply U.S. and European thinking, it is tough to be competitive in China," he quipped.

"What attracted us to move from an MNC to a local company is passion, speed, and the decisions that you can make when you see an opportunity." Jeffrey explains his move: "Companies like Mengniu are catching up and learning. You start seeing a hybrid of things [adopted] from the MNCs; governance has improved, but we remain fast, innovative and passionate." At the leadership level at Mengniu, half of his team came from MNCs, with the others promoted through the ranks at Mengniu.

His adds an intriguing remark: "Local company leaders are not too democratic. But sometimes, too much democracy in the system makes things very, very difficult…"

I take this opportunity to probe him on how he manages Western and Chinese stakeholders at Mengniu. "What are the areas of disagreement?" I ask. "The overall strategy is aligned," he replies. He spent four or five months developing the strategy to get alignment across shareholders and among the Board before joining. Where there is difference is in the investment time horizon. "COFCO is even more long-term because we believe that we will be doing something good for China," he explains. "When we think of important strategies, we always remind ourselves that we need a role in China, and this role will require long term investment."

"Relatively speaking, Danone and other shareholders are focused more on shorter-term efficiencies and operational improvements. They are complementary to a certain extent." Jeffrey's positive framing of both organizations underlines his diplomatic skills.

I turn my attention next to the potential for improvement within the three key areas highlighted by Jeffrey when he first took over. "On a scale of 1 to 10, what is our progress in each of these?"

"Sourcing and working on operational efficiency were the first measures we took. These were the low-hanging fruits," Jeffrey reflects. "We are now very, very good here and I'd rank this as 100% done."

Next is brand and innovation to drive growth. "When you have growth, you have time to fix issues!" Mengniu is selling 30 billion packets of products each year, so the delivery system is already in place. They are working on the "engines" (e.g., more nutrition, more functional ingredients) to drive premiumization.

The third is Route to Market (RTM). He explains that RTM requires an entire change in the system; it requires a lot of time and room to maneuver. For example, if you cut off one distributor, you can lose one month of distributor sales. "But if you have strong brand and strong innovation, with growth, you have time to fix RTM." Such is the kind of logical and clear roadmap that Jeffrey brings to fixing operational issues.

Jeffrey rates Mengniu's progress on these other two points as 75% and 50% along the way. "We have a clear roadmap. We know how much time we need for the transformation."

I steer the conversation to areas where Mengniu still has lots to do. On Environmental and Sustainability issues, whilst Mengniu is already a leader compared to domestic peers, it still lags far behind global peers. "What are Mengniu's targets and timeline for reducing carbon emissions?"

Jeffrey acknowledges this is an area they need to tackle. Mengniu is using technology and digitization to address this. His hands become animated as he describes how they are studying the carbon footprint of each of their activities, from raw milk sourcing to manufacturing to logistics. "We will know the exact carbon footprint of each of our activities by the end of 2021. And through our digital system, we can improve farming efficiency by knowing the optimal feed for each cow." He takes a sip of his lemon water.

Given the even more potent greenhouse effects of methane than carbon dioxide, I challenge Jeffrey on whether the dairy industry would become the next fossil fuel industry. The feeding system is an important focus for them. "Probiotics for cows are also important." They are working on probiotics to significantly improve the cows' digestive systems in order to reduce methane production. "How interesting and totally logical!" I exclaim. "Since humans eat probiotics to improve gut health, it makes total sense to apply it to animals too!" Jeffrey continues, "Plant-based products is another area. We are working on mimicking the taste of milk and developing products that are plant-based but taste just like milk. There is a lot of new technology in synthetic biology for designing proteins…"

I can connect the dots from Jeffrey's science background to his focus on using technology at Mengniu to drive product innovation and push forward on environmental and sustainability issues. In Mengniu's case, ESG issues and long-term strategy are joined at the hip.

I am conscious of time, but before we wrap up, I ask Jeffrey about his impressions of Overlook. "How is Overlook different, if at all, from other investors you have interacted with?"

He replies readily with his top-of-mind impressions. "First thing obviously is that you are very long term; that is important. Second is you really look into the future, what the future will look like – not just about today's performance, but to see how the company will evolve in the longer term in terms of strategy and team."

As Overlook celebrates its 30th anniversary, "What comments and advice would you give to us so that we can remain successful investors for the future decades?"

Jeffrey smiles as he replies, "There is a huge opportunity in China. Spending good quality time in China to understand what has changed is important – where the market is going; what is the speed." He adds, "Overlook should open an office in China." I engage him on which city he would recommend to locate our office and reflect on his answers.

Jeffrey has been generous with his time and I notice he has not eaten his lunch yet. We agree that we will have a proper lunch together the next time we meet up. I have been so engaged in our conversation that I too have barely eaten my lunch. As we wrap up the call, I taste my curry chicken, which was cooked using Mengniu's "Just" yogurt in place of coconut milk. The taste is just as authentic, although the texture would have been better if Mengniu had a thicker, Greek-style yogurt. My mind explores the future product opportunities available to Mengniu to cater to the Food Service segment, and I imagine in the future what a Mengniu plant-based milk might taste like.

Menu

- Homemade curry chicken cooked with Mengniu's "Just" Yogurt: $2.

- Panna cotta made with Mengniu's "Milk Deluxe" and drizzled with Mengniu's "Jujube" Yogurt: $2.

- Warm lemon water.

Hong Kong, Our Home

Moderated by William Leung

If Hong Kong were ruined in our hands, we would become sinners of the nation. This will not happen.

— ZHU RONGJI,
upon landing in Hong Kong in November 2002

Biography of William Leung

William is a Partner at Overlook Investments and a member of the Investment Committee. When I think about William, my overriding wish is that I could be like him, and not just because he is nearly 25 years younger than me. He is encyclopedic about Asian public companies and insightful on the nuances of investment opportunities that often determine the difference between success and failure. A Hong Kong local, William experienced the 1997/98 Asian Crisis and the 2000 Tech Bubble Burst firsthand as a summer intern at Barings, where he first met James Squire.

William has more than 20 years of investment experience under his belt, with invaluable experience in China that benefits Overlook. William is soft spoken and well read on investments, with an incredible passion for stock picking. His favorite weekend pastimes include reading financial history books and corporate annual reports from his huge collections at home.

William suggested that his contribution to *The Model* be to moderate a panel comprised of the members of the Board of Advisors on a subject titled, "Hong Kong, Our Home." With so much being written about Hong Kong, I think hearing the views of people who have spent many decades in Hong Kong accumulating wisdom and insights provides new perspectives. They have lived the history of modern Hong Kong and I am pleased that they have agreed to share their thoughts with us.

The Panel

Allow me to briefly introduce each participant in the discussion.

Dr. Marc Faber is author of *The Gloom, Boom & Doom Report*. He has been Asia's most prolific commentator on global financial markets over the past four decades. Marc is a true independent thinker, an instinctive contrarian, a successful investor and a generous philanthropist. Without a doubt, Overlook would not be in business today were it not for Marc's support 30 years ago. One of my favorite meals every year is our dinner at the Grand Hyatt the night before Overlook's annual Board of Advisors meeting. Marc has been a member of the Board of Advisors since inception.

Terry Fok is one of Hong Kong's preeminent stock pickers. His investment style combines creativity, detailed knowledge of companies, an eye on deep value, and patience. I met Terry 35 years ago and quickly learned that he is not to be underestimated. Over the past several decades, one of my great joys has been sharing lunch with Terry at the China Club, a restaurant in the old Bank of China Building, where the two of us are oblivious to the world as we talk about stocks. Terry has been on the Overlook Board of Advisors since 2002.

David Halperin is one of the senior American lawyers in Hong Kong and has lived in Hong Kong for over 40 years. David is a former partner at Coudert Brothers, the source of all great American lawyers in Hong Kong. I first met David 30 years ago as I leaned up against the Xerox machine at Coudert Brothers waiting for my legal documents to be copied on the night before I left on Overlook's first overseas marketing trip. David has mentored hundreds of young Americans in Hong Kong including Joe Tsai, vice chairman of Alibaba. I have also had many opportunities to enjoy David's platform for mentoring: mid-week dinner parties at his beautifully decorated apartment, where he brings together an interesting and eclectic selection of people. David has been on the Board of Advisors since 2004.

Aubrey Li. I met Aubrey 37 years ago when I first arrived in Hong Kong and joined a fledging Brown University Club in the city. I quickly learned that Aubrey, an investment banker by profession, is one of the great gentlemen of Hong Kong. Some of my favorite nights in Hong Kong have been spent with Aubrey in a private suite at the Happy Valley racetrack for Wednesday night horse racing, which Aubrey so generously hosted. Over time, it never surprised me that Aubrey was on the Board of some of my favorite companies, such as Café de Coral. Aubrey has been endlessly loyal to Overlook, a source of great advice for many years and a member of our Board of Advisors since 2002.

Mike Lonergan. I first met Mike about 35 years ago when we both worked at First Pacific. He was in the accounting department with an expat package; I was in an investment arm and paying my own rent. After many years apart, a candidate for the CFO role at Overlook turned me down but suggested I reach out to Mike. That was the beginning of my luck working alongside Mike. He worked as CFO and CEO of Overlook for 12 years. When Mike came on board, he began taking lunch in the conference room. More and more people began to join him and lively conversations ensued as we talked about the issues of the day. It strengthened the culture at Overlook and the tradition still continues today. Mike is also the inventor of the Mike Lonergan Method of Negotiating, a technique that is eminently useful. Upon retirement from Overlook, he started a third career as a philanthropist. He has been a member of the Overlook Board of Advisors since 2018.

Hong Kong, Our Home

William: The past five decades have been a very prosperous period for Hong Kong when the city has evolved to become a key international finance center in Asia.

No other major cities in the world have experienced more booms and busts in the past 50 years than Hong Kong – the 1967 Riot, the Oil Crisis of the 1970s, the Crash in 1987, the Handover in 1997, the Asian Financial Crisis in 1997–98, SARS

in 2003, the Global Financial Crisis in 2008, as well as the recent social unrest. Yet, the city has flourished and shown its resilience through tough times.

What has made Hong Kong so successful despite all the changes and challenges over the years?

Terry, may we start with you?

Terry: Of course, William. Thank you.

I would say Hong Kong has always been a place where people get together to make money. The reasons are the low taxes, the legal system, and the fact that we are part of China.

Also, the fixed exchange rate of the Hong Kong dollar to the U.S. dollar has helped enormously in providing financial stability.

William: Excellent points, Terry. David?

David: First, Hong Kong's work ethic. It's always impressed me that banks, law firms, and companies are open on Saturdays. It's a standard working day. That's not true in most other places. Hong Kong is a hard-working city.

Second, there are no exchange controls here, so there's free movement of capital.

Third, no corruption. The ICAC [Independent Commission Against Corruption] was established in 1974, and corruption has largely been eliminated in Hong Kong.

Fourth, Hong Kong became an attractive place for foreigners to come and seek their fortunes in the Far East. Hong Kong is the only city in China that has English as an official language.

Mike: I think Hong Kong's work ethic is the big thing. I came from London to Hong Kong and noticed right away that people here didn't leave the office until 7:30–8:00 at night, and work Saturday mornings, too.

William: People in Hong Kong walk very fast as if they are running.

One second seems even too much to waste. I would also add honesty and integrity to the point on work ethics.

Aubrey: Geography is certainly important, including Hong Kong's proximity to China, and the fact that over ten Asian countries can be reached within a four- or five-hour flight.

I think the other main factor is the free trading environment in Hong Kong that has attracted so many entrepreneurs. In the 50s and the 60s an influx of immigrants came from Mainland China – talented people, major industrialists and senior bankers from Shanghai. Also, Hong Kong has always attracted people and businesses from all over the world. People here are so business savvy. It's easy to do business here.

In the 1990s China realized that it needed expertise and capital for investment in China businesses, and Hong Kong was the perfect place for that. Call it luck or destiny, it was just the right place at the right time.

Marc: I think it was a huge advantage that Hong Kong was not a democracy. I think that if Hong Kong had been a democracy, it would never have become as prosperous as it has. The British brought a legal system that was honest and a bureaucracy that was efficient and small. With very little government intervention, Hong Kong has a high degree of entrepreneurship, of people who wanted to work hard and do business. That, in my opinion, was a very important factor in making Hong Kong prosperous.

For any foreigner coming to Asia, where would you like to be sent? Taipei? Seoul? Ugly cities. Singapore? There's nothing special about Singapore. But Hong Kong, with its topography and the sea and the harbor, is a stunningly beautiful place.

Hong Kong's Special Appeal

William: I'm a Hong Kong local, born and raised here before going to Canada and the U.S. for higher education. Looking back, for me to come back for my family and for my career was easily one of my best life decisions.

Foreign talent has contributed a fair share in the success story of Hong Kong. I am always fascinated by personal stories of the expatriates. What most attracted you to come to Hong Kong in the first place, and why did you stay?

Marc: I think I realized the economic potential of Asia and Hong Kong. Whereas in the Western world there was a high degree of regulation, Hong Kong was a free dealing place, with enormous freedoms which rewarded people who were prepared to work hard.

Based in Hong Kong you can easily access the whole of Asia. Hong Kong is the center of Asia, and it is a great place to live as well.

When I first arrived, Asia was very poor. And now to see the changes! Everything has moved ahead in infrastructure, freedom of commerce, and economic growth.

Everything from the day I arrived in Hong Kong, even crossing the harbor on the Star Ferry, has been an incredible experience. And not just Hong Kong, the experience in all of Asia has been unforgettable.

Terry: It's because of the opening up of China. I remember I had some U.S. clients telling me China is like the Wild West of the United States. It was really exciting. My analysts kept telling me the money was falling from the sky.

David: To me, Hong Kong seemed like an adventure, more interesting than remaining in New York and being one of 200–300 lawyers in a big law firm. It felt like pioneering a frontier. Hong Kong is next to China, but was an easier place to live, and an easy place to do business. I remember in the

80s documenting hundreds of loans to governments and corporations all across Asia. It was exciting to be at the forefront of financing Asia's growth.

Mike: After I qualified as a chartered accountant in London with Ernst & Young in 1986, I was offered the opportunity of an overseas posting for two years. I chose Hong Kong. My wife and I had never been to the Far East before, so everything was new. On our first day here, we wandered down to the harbor front and were just blown away by the feeling of the place, the energy and excitement.

When it came time to go back, my wife and I both decided that London wasn't really for us any longer.

William: The night view of Hong Kong is simply too seductive. I am reminded that Richard told me a similar story of walking to Victoria Harbour on the night before he and Dee were going to travel into China for four months and having the same realization that they were not returning to America.

David: Hong Kong is also one of the safest cities in the world.

Terry: Tokyo, Taipei, Singapore, and Hong Kong – the four safest cities, most modern cities, in the world.

Aubrey: I moved back to Hong Kong in 1980 and it wasn't a difficult decision. I liked the free entrepreneurial atmosphere, the population of hard-working businesspeople. Hong Kong's supercharged efficiency is next to none. And the cultural experience for expats, locally and regionally, is interesting. Western expats just fall in love with Hong Kong.

In the mid-80s, East Asia Warburg, where I worked, was being considered to act as a financial advisor to a major trading conglomerate. The chairman was Hong Kong Chinese but didn't speak English. We had prepared a presentation and even brought one of our directors in from London. I was translating, and as the meeting began the owner said to our expat managing director, "I like your face. In feng shui, you have a good honest reliable face. You are appointed." It was only a 15-minute meeting. It was typical of the convergence of different cultures in those days.

Hong Kong's Future

William: With the handover of Hong Kong to China in 1997, many people were concerned about what might happen to Hong Kong. Doomsayers predicted the demise of Hong Kong, as they had previously in the 80s and the 90s, but they were proven wrong. Today, however, doubts have once again arisen about Hong Kong's future.

Let's examine what changes Hong Kong is navigating in today's rapidly changing geopolitical and business landscapes. Are Hong Kong's many advantages intact? Will Hong Kong continue to be successful as in the past?

Mike: I have always been skeptical that Hong Kong would be granted full democracy while China didn't have it. In the period before 2012, Chinese leaders did create some optimism that they might be moving towards a partially democratic system; but since then, such hopes have been extinguished.

David: I think it's fair to point out that every country has some form of sedition law. So I don't feel excessively worried about the new National Security Law corrupting the legal system. I think the courts will continue to follow trusted common law for most cases, unless there is an element that touches on national security.

Terry: Things were going well for Hong Kong between 2003 and 2012, but then, with the change in political leadership in China, things are not as clear for most Hong Kong families, especially those who are not rich. Many may leave Hong Kong. Otherwise, politics aside, Hong Kong is still a good place.

Aubrey: I think the biggest change has been the growing influence of China. Before the Handover, Hong Kong was basically a relatively small regional financial center. After 1997, Hong Kong became the bridge for international capital into China, opening up huge potential for the city. At the same time, as China opened, Shanghai became the major domestic financial center of China. Hong Kong's role is now as the *international* financial center for China, and that role should remain intact. Hong Kong is still the leading conduit to attract international investment and foreign talent.

With free movement of capital, the rule of law, and a diverse talent pool, Hong Kong still has an edge which nobody can replace right now. But we have to play our cards right, and we cannot stand still.

Risks for Hong Kong? Income inequality. Local young people feel frustrated building a career. They can't afford to buy a property. They blame China for these problems, and this has led to anti-China sentiment. For people to stay, Hong Kong has to prove itself to be an attractive place to live and work and to build a career. Hong Kong did just that in the 80s and the 90s, but we have to prove it again.

Marc: From a professional point of view, I am quite positive about Hong Kong. I don't take a very negative view of the National Security Law. You just have to know that in Hong Kong, you shouldn't walk around with banners that say, "Take down Xi Jinping" and so on. I think the opportunities are still here, but they are different than they used to be. In life and in business there are always doors that close. One door closes and you have to open another. This is a question of attitude, of constantly learning, and of faith in the future.

If I have one regret, it is that I didn't learn Mandarin. To be based in Hong Kong, one has to be able to communicate fluently with Mainland Chinese people in Mandarin.

William: Marc, it sounds like you have a positive view on Hong Kong's future, but with a caveat?

Marc: Yes, I do, provided the people in Hong Kong realize the change in the position of Hong Kong, and provided they no longer live under the "China needs Hong Kong" mindset. I've always said that China doesn't need Hong Kong, it is Hong Kong that needs China.

Will People Leave Hong Kong?

William: Hong Kong previously had two periods of population exodus: after the social unrest in 1967, and then in the years leading up to the 1997 Handover. Rumor is that as much as 10% of Hong Kong's population emigrated during the 80s and the 90s, though many decided to move back to Hong Kong later.

With the recent social unrest and the new National Security Law, etc., how significant could an upcoming exodus be? What percentage of the population might emigrate, and why?

David: I would guess something like 5–7% may decide to leave. I think that those who leave will be replaced by talented Mainland Chinese, who will choose to move to Hong Kong.

Marc: I'd say some people will leave, maybe 10–15%, but an equal number will come.

The people who leave will be those who complain about high property costs and about China. On balance, I think a rejuvenation of the population is actually favorable.

Mike: Less than 5%. I think Hong Kong people are pragmatic, and that they will adjust to the new reality. I don't think the exodus would be huge.

Terry: I would say 7%. Half a million in five years. People change eventually. Some of the young generation will become Singaporean. Or if they go to the U.K. or the U.S., they will become British Chinese or American Chinese.

Aubrey: I would have thought 5%, but it will be more gradual than the 1997 migration. People were panicking then, but this time people are not panicking. Many have decent jobs and are not going to just pack up and go. Young people are watching and keeping their eyes open. Also, populism and career prospects in other countries, such as the U.S., can be a deterrent.

One of the differences between now and 1997 is that Chinese companies now have a much bigger presence in Hong Kong. Chinese companies are setting up international headquarters in Hong Kong. It's the ideal place to take care of international business. It is already happening. There was an article in the newspaper recently that China Resources Group, a SOE, bought 50 flats for their Hong Kong-based staff.

William: My guesstimate would be less than 5%. I am amazed at just how resilient Hong Kong property prices have been, especially in the past 2–3 years. Such resilience points to future strengths that most people might have underestimated.

Hong Kong and the Greater Bay Area

William: Any discussions about Hong Kong's economic future must include the Greater Bay Area (GBA). It is only reasonable to expect that Hong Kong will become more and more integrated with the GBA cities. Hong Kong is already becoming much more interconnected with the GBA by transportation infrastructure including new rail lines, roads, and bridges connecting GBA cities and Hong Kong.

Will Hong Kong be economically overtaken by Shanghai or Shenzhen? Will Hong Kong become more important to China, or less relevant?

Terry: I can see a lot of changes, and now people are starting to refer to Hong Kong as Southern Shenzhen. Not Hong Kong, but Southern Shenzhen.

David: Young people should widen their view to see the opportunities and advantages throughout the Greater Bay Area.

A disadvantage for young people in Hong Kong is that they do not speak Mandarin fluently. If you only speak Cantonese, you're not competitive with your Mainland counterparts.

We still have Hong Kong's legal system. If you have a dispute, do you want to have it heard by a judge in Shenzhen or Zhuhai? I don't think so. People throughout the entire region will always have a greater trust in Hong Kong courts and prefer to arbitrate disputes in Hong Kong.

Mike: I think it's inevitable that Hong Kong gets subsumed into the Greater Bay Area. The infrastructure build-up is already happening. With Hong Kong's position and status in the world, I don't see any incentive for China to destroy what's already here. I think Hong Kong will remain an important city for China.

Marc: If you look at the history of independent cities, they were all eventually absorbed by a larger entity or an empire. Salzburg, as an example, was an independent city in the Middle Ages, and then later became an important cultural center. Venice, also, once had a very important role in trade, similar to Hong Kong today as the gateway between China and the rest of the world.

You ask whether Shanghai or Shenzhen will overtake Hong Kong economically. They have already done so in some sectors of the economy. That's capitalism. Hong Kong just has to play its cards right and it can be an important city in a huge empire.

Aubrey: GBA represents perhaps the greatest opportunity for Hong Kong for the next 20 years. Hong Kong can contribute with international experience, professional expertise, finance, business services, and corporate development. Hong Kong continues to develop as a base for international business in the GBA. We need more young people to go to the Greater Bay Area to work and to seek opportunities. The challenge is up to Hong Kong itself – the Hong Kong Government and the Hong Kong people.

William: It is statistically true that the importance of Hong Kong has diminished over time, if measured by the city's GDP as a percent of China's overall GDP. However, one could argue that Hong Kong has actually become more relevant for its key role as the gateway for international investment into and out of China. Hong Kong now accounts for about two-thirds of FDI [foreign direct investment] flows into and out of China, much higher than ten years ago.

Here is an example: The Stock Connect Program, launched in 2014, has brought lucrative opportunities to the financial industry in Hong Kong. More importantly, international investors can now directly invest into A-Shares under the program. The Stock Connect also helped the A-Shares to be included in major stock indices around the world. The economic benefits are mutual between China and Hong Kong. This is why Hong Kong remains highly relevant and cannot be replaced anytime soon.

Chinese Capital Flow via Hong Kong

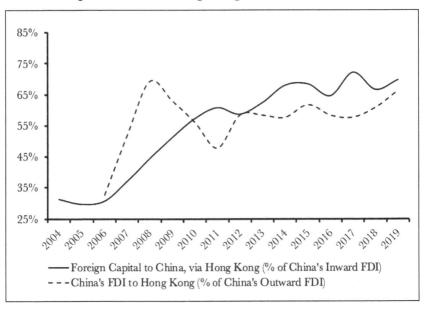

Sources: BIS, Overlook.

Observations on Overlook

William: Overlook and our investors have benefited tremendously from the diverse talent pool available in Hong Kong. Today, Overlook is proud to say that we are half Asian,

half non-Asian, half female, and half male. This is not something one could easily replicate in other Asian cities. We believe that a diverse and skilled labor pool is one of Hong Kong's, and Overlook's, many advantages.

We'd like to hear from you, as our advisors, and all long-time friends of Overlook, on what you have observed about Overlook over the past 30 years and what has impressed you most.

Mike: Yes, diversity is a fundamental principle for Overlook.

I would say Overlook's consistent application of its Investment Philosophy has been everything.

Also, Overlook is a unique organization, examples of which are the ability to establish unique strengths, like cutting fees, returning capital, establishing a system for succession planning. Many companies fail to do these things.

Overlook's willingness to be independent-minded and not be influenced by short-term market trends. Overlook is always planning five to ten years out, which makes a huge difference in the way you run a business.

There's one other thing as well. We work hard on the administration, management, and client service side of the business. That's one more building block in how the business should be run.

Terry: The Overlook Model. That's been the key to success.

Overlook doesn't try to grow the fund just to make more fees. Also, Richard is willing to have a smaller piece in a bigger pie by sharing ownership of the firm with his executives.

David: Overlook has a way of developing personal relationships with the owners and executives of the companies in which they invest. Because they respect Overlook, they listen, and Overlook can influence companies on important matters.

Mike: Overlook may not get to influence management at all of our investments, but our advice is often heard, and that has certainly made a contribution to our returns. Persistence is the key.

David: Yes, Mike, true. I'm also impressed by the relatively small number of companies in the portfolio and the low turnover of the portfolio. It is a focused approach to investing.

Aubrey: I see the Investment Philosophy, the disciplined process, and the unselfish culture as Overlook's greatest strengths.

Overlook is a real Hong Kong success story – the team-oriented culture, minimum bureaucracy, and flat management structure, which is contrary to the idea of always having to build a big business.

The other thing that has really impressed me is not being greedy, which is a rarity in Hong Kong. It's a nice way to run a business.

Marc: One of the strengths of Overlook is that the focus has always been on making money for the clients. This is unlike many fund management companies and investment banks where the focus is on making money for themselves. That was not the aim of Overlook at any time. I repeat: not at any time.

The primary objective at Overlook is to make money for clients. If the clients make money, then they will stay and the others will invest. I think that client focus to deliver capital-weighted returns is a very great strength of the Overlook team.

Controlling the size of the fund, also. Overlook has always had the view that they don't want a huge inflow of money when the fund has done well in strong markets. When markets become overheated, the firm has even given back capital to investors. On the other hand, when markets are down, Overlook may accept more capital so as to take advantage of opportunities.

The firm has remained very focused on one fund in Asia. They could have expanded by starting a European or Latin American fund, but they didn't do that. They stayed focused on what they know and do best. I think clients value that focus.

Twenty years ago, Overlook had hardly any investments in China. Then the team realized, long before other investors, that Chinese companies had become better managed, that there was a huge market in China with huge potential. Going from almost no investments in China 20 years ago to having 50–60% in China was a very courageous and successful step.

William: That's very comprehensive, Marc. In my opinion, Overlook's ability and willingness to sell securities is one major strength.

How Could Overlook Improve?

William: Along the 30-year journey since its founding in 1991, Overlook has of course made its share of mistakes, and we try to learn from our mistakes. In your view, how could Overlook improve in the years ahead?

Mike: I think Overlook's success speaks for itself. I don't know what else you could do!

Aubrey: One area Overlook should never stop learning is in the qualitative assessment of people, be they business owners, management teams, staff, friends, etc.

Marc: For Overlook, if the firm remains client-oriented and transparent, I believe Overlook will continue to do well.

The key is to avoid huge mistakes [laughs]. And so far – and I've known Richard since he started this company – this has been avoided through prudence, patience, and, as I said, lack of personal greed.

David: I sometimes wonder why Overlook doesn't seem particularly interested in technology stocks, which have become such a factor in the markets in the last 15 years. Those companies have different dynamics that don't always fit comfortably within The Overlook Model, but I've wondered whether there could be more interest in that sector.

William: Many internet companies have no earnings. All three internet companies Overlook currently holds – Alibaba, NetEase, and Tencent – generate very solid cash flows and high operating returns which can be properly valued. That sets those three stocks apart from some of the other tech high-flyers. We don't swing at every pitch. We just have to make sure that we don't miss if the fat pitch comes.

Terry: It appears that all Overlook executives more or less belong to the same school of investing. You might need to have different people for brainstorming purposes.

Overlook's Next 30 Years

William: Please share your vision for Overlook's next 30 years. What do you think the firm needs to do in order to meet or exceed its past performance?

Terry: Why change if you can keep this Model compounding at 14% a year? To me, I don't think major changes are necessary, except perhaps minor adjustments along the way.

Mike: It's about adding to the tools as we learn more, little tweaks like adding pricing power to the way we evaluate companies. Otherwise, why would we change?

David: Perhaps if technology is becoming a more important part of our lives and it's something that younger people understand, adding people to the team who have a particular competence in technology would seem useful and relevant for the next coming decades.

Marc: Most companies need to think not about getting better, but about staying as good as they are. If things in the past have proven to be very good, why change? Remain client focused. Focus on the business the way it has been. Invest in a limited number of companies and stay in close touch with those investments. I don't think there is a need to change anything.

And yes, technology will become important, but maybe more important will be that people have to eat. I'm not saying you ought to invest all your money in food stocks but keep a balanced portfolio. I would do exactly what you've done and stay the way you are, especially in the Investment Philosophy, in remaining humble, and not wanting to over-expand in bubbles.

Aubrey: I think that The Overlook Model shouldn't change much.

When more and more Chinese companies are worth following, it may well be that you will want a research office in China. Having a local office gives you a chance to hear gossip and insights on people and companies.

We can extrapolate what's been happening over the past 30 years. I think Asia will be a much bigger investment market and will become more and more China focused. For example, within MSCI Global, China weighting is now about 5%, and the U.S., about 58%. That doesn't correctly reflect the size of the two economies.

If Overlook keeps the focus on Asia, you're playing to your strength. Overlook has a reputation for its Asia focus. Stay within Asia, expand with Asia's growth.

William: This has been an interesting and insightful discussion. All of us at Overlook thank you for your time today and for all that you have done for Overlook as members of the Board of Advisors.

Perhaps we can close this discussion about Hong Kong with a memorable and fitting quote from Aubrey Li, who, during the dark days of the Asian Financial Crisis in 1998, reminded me that: "No one ever won selling Hong Kong short."

ESG: The Climate Divergence

Contributed by
Richard H. Lawrence, Jr.

Illegitimi non carborundum, often translated as "Don't let the bastards grind you down."

— MOCK-LATIN APHORISM

"No Problem"

IN THE EARLY 1990s, China was just beginning to industrialize. In Guangdong Province, across the border from Hong Kong, new industrial estates were being rushed into development on land that for millennia had been agricultural. Nearby hills were being flattened, literally by hand, with workers hanging by ropes loosening soil from the face of the hill. As the soil dropped to the base of the hill, it was loaded onto trucks and spread in a six-foot layer over the old rice paddies and orange plantations, creating a base for new factories.

I visited one of those factories in 1993. It was owned by a Hong Kong-listed company that made paints and solvents. I had previously met with the company managers, who were proud of having aggressively lowered costs by locating production in China and opening new sales opportunities in mainland markets. They invited me to see their China operations and offered to make arrangements.

The factory manager was all smiles and politeness as he greeted me. Tea was served in the offices. Then he gave me the factory tour.

You are familiar with the smell of spray paint, yes? Powerful. Dangerous. Entering the factory floor, it hit like a punch: the chemical miasma, thick and choking, stinging one's throat and eyes. Dozens of unprotected workers were busy around the vats and the machinery. There was no visible ventilation system but for a few fans placed here and there, and two small open windows. "Aren't the chemical vapors dangerous to your employees?" I asked. "Oh, no problem," the manager said. "We only allow employees to work here for two years. They become addicted to the fumes, so we make them leave after two years. So, no problem."

We exited by a side door, next to a drainage culvert leading from the factory to a nearby stream. It was streaked with a rainbow of slow-moving paint sludge. Toxic waste. I pointed to it. "It's OK," the manager said, "No problem."

Back in Hong Kong, the company got an earful from me, said they would look into it… Nobody really cared; it was 1993 in Asia. We did not invest in the company, of course, but the bar of acting responsibly for me and for Overlook was forever and indelibly raised because, while China and the world may have come a long way since 1993, "No problem" is not a solution.

Environment, Social and Governance Responsibilities

From our March 2020 Quarterly Report:

Given the heightened coverage of ESG efforts by investors, financial institutions, and the press, I wanted to take this opportunity to review Overlook's commitment to ESG, which started 28 years ago and has been a part of Overlook's culture for the past three decades. Overlook's investors should instantly recognize our commitment to Governance (G) and Social (S). However, we have never publicly discussed our work on the Environment (E). Pulling the curtain back on our E work is the objective of this letter. But first, let me provide a few examples of our commitment to the G & S issues.

Modern Finance Technology (MFT). I think it is fair to say that Overlook has been fighting for improved corporate governance and capital management since our inception in Marc Faber's office 28 years ago. While our efforts to enhance Asian governance are private and confidential by rule, we believe that MFT has been a significant contributor to Overlook's performance.

Our commitment to governance also extends internally to Overlook. We initiated the transition to second- and third-generation leadership over nine years ago precisely because it was in the long-term interests of all Overlook investors.

Overlook's commitment to diversity has helped strengthen all aspects of our business. Overlook today is half female, half male; half Asian and half Western. Geographically, my Asian colleagues come from all over Asia, and the Westerners come from all around the world. Our median age is 41 years old. Diversity is a core strength of the firm.

We have avoided what we call "Bottom of the Pyramid" companies for almost two decades. These are the low margin, high capital

investment intensity, heavily indebted companies that lack
the resources to take care of the societal and governance
challenges they face.

Asia is not perfect, but is making steady progress on S & G issues;
and we believe the global ESG Movement will further improve
conditions for all stakeholders over the coming decade.

ENVIRONMENT: THIS IS THE FIGHT
OF THE NEXT DECADE

Without diminishing the importance of S & G, the threat caused
by climate change to our portfolio will be one of the big fights
our companies face over the coming decade. And I would like to
discuss Overlook's decade-long effort on climate change below.

RICHARD LAWRENCE'S JOURNEY

In 2005, my family and I began building fuel-efficient cookstoves in
rural Honduras. When a client learned of this work, he introduced
me to Jeremy Grantham, founder of GMO and the finance industry's
pioneering climate activist. After our first meeting, Jeremy donated
US$ 10,000 to our fledging stove non-profit. On subsequent trips
to Boston, Jeremy graciously allocated time to sit with me and talk
about the world. We discussed cookstoves; his work at EDF, WWF,
and Rare; the voluntary carbon market; the cap-and-trade system;
population control; the stock market; running a fund management
business; China's response to climate change; and more. On one
visit he quietly suggested I read Lord Stern's *The Economics of
Climate Change*, a book published in 2006 that opened my eyes to
the global nature of the climate threat. And on one of my next trips
to Boston, Jeremy agreed to match my investment to appropriately
capitalize Proyecto Mirador, the cookstove project.

From modest beginnings, The Grantham Foundation and the
Lawrence Family have built 240,000 fuel-efficient cookstoves
in poor rural households in Honduras and, more recently, in
Guatemala and Nicaragua. Quite incredibly, and unexpectedly for

both Jeremy and me, the non-profit, Proyecto Mirador, has self-funded its growth through the sale of Gold Standard certified carbon credits. The carbon certification process at Proyecto Mirador has provided us an education over the past 13 years on the elements of high-quality carbon emission reductions. What is the significance of "additionality"? Are the stated emission reductions truly "additional"? Have corners been cut in the emission reduction calculations? Is the baseline emission level accurate or inflated? What conflicts of interest exist in the transaction of carbon credits?

I tell this rather long-winded story as my relationship with Jeremy served as the basis for Overlook's understanding of, and perspective on, climate change. Without my experience with Jeremy, Overlook might well be like many other fund managers: blind to the risks and opportunities that investors will confront in the coming decade. Thankfully, we are not blind.

OVERLOOK'S JOURNEY

14 years ago, Overlook and all of its employees embraced a policy of offsetting our carbon emissions with Gold Standard carbon credits from Proyecto Mirador. Honestly, the offsetting idea began as an initiative to encourage my colleagues to give back to society. However, as you might imagine, the analysts questioned the reality of climate change and the validity of carbon credits. In the process, they accelerated their education about and concern over the climate threat.

10 years ago, Overlook's Investment Committee officially adopted an annual policy of excluding one or more industries from our investible universe for E reasons. James and I first eliminated coal mining, moved on to fossil fuels, and most recently outlawed the extraction of metals. As we took these actions, we learned that offsetting carbon emissions and divesting from high-emission industries are only initial steps.

The more significant benefit from these actions was to raise Overlook's collective awareness of the attractive investment opportunities created by the energy transition. And contrary to public opinion, climate change is not all downside. Our investment in 2013 into shares of China Yangtze Power Company, Asia's largest renewable energy company and China's lowest-cost electricity producer, confirmed that climate change offers upside for investors.

"PART OF THE SOLUTION" OR "PART OF THE PROBLEM"?

Fundamentally, Overlook considers the IPCC goal of a 50% reduction in global emissions by 2030 to be a very ambitious and largely unrealistic target. Thus, the multiple threats posed by climate change to our portfolio companies will continue, if not accelerate.

Overlook's belief is that over the coming decade, investors will judge nearly all public companies on their commitment and ability to reduce the carbon intensity of their operations and the planet. Investors will designate companies as either "part of the solution" (the "Solution") or "part of the problem" (the "Problem"). And share valuations will reflect these judgments. So, what makes a company qualify for Solution status?

QUALITIES OF SOLUTION COMPANIES

Three components form the core of Overlook's analysis of corporate behavior on the Environment. Many Overlook investors could reasonably criticize Overlook for this narrow scope; but, in our view, the most urgent problem is to reduce the excessive accumulation of carbon dioxide in the atmosphere. We believe that Overlook's adoption of this methodology gives us tangible and valuable investment insights by helping identify the future Solutions. We must have the following:

» Clear understanding of the long-term impact of climate change on current and future portfolio holdings. Why is each holding a Solution, not a Problem? Our work includes analysis of stranded assets and liabilities, physical climate risks, transition risks, and the evolution of specific companies within a world where disruption will accelerate. We must have an open mind to understand that Solution companies will emerge from many industries not immediately apparent to investors today.

» Detailed corporate emission data that is transparent, verifiable, and calculated according to global best accounting practices. While this sounds easy, carbon accounting is extraordinarily complicated with many hidden pitfalls. Corporations can manipulate their emission footprint and disclosures in a host of ways that are difficult for average investors to uncover or comprehend. Technical knowledge of carbon accounting is a must for Overlook to arrive at accurate conclusions.

» Clear involvement of each CEO and Board of Directors in establishing science-based plans to reduce carbon intensity and allocate capital expenditures in a manner that is consistent with a path to 1.5 degrees Celsius, the Paris Agreement's long-term temperature goal. It is not enough to passively delegate this effort to a CFO or Chief Sustainability Officer. Overlook wants transparent involvement by the CEO and the Board of Directors.

Our analysis diverges from the current standards of the investment management industry. We consider much of the industry's ESG analysis to be nonsensical and simply designed to help investors tick boxes and cross ts on every aspect of ESG. Again, we do not want to diminish the importance of water, wage equality, air pollution, or other S&G factors. But in our view, they do not pose the same magnitude of risk as climate change.

THE CLIMATE BIFURCATION

Overlook believes that being "part of the problem" will be expensive for investors who own those stocks and being "part of the solution" will reward investors. We call this The Climate Bifurcation. Evidence of this divergence is already evident in share prices and we share a few examples below.

Total Return: CYPC vs China Coal Companies (10 Year)

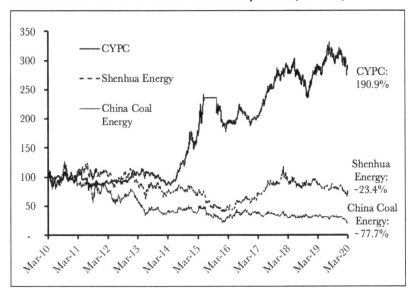

Rebased to 100 and adjusted for dividends.
Source: Bloomberg.

Total Return: Orsted vs KEPCO (Since IPO)

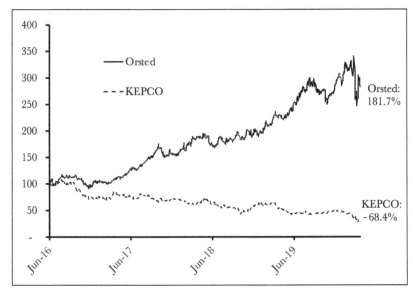

Rebased to 100 and adjusted for dividends.
Source: Bloomberg.

Total Return: Toyota vs GM (Since IPO)

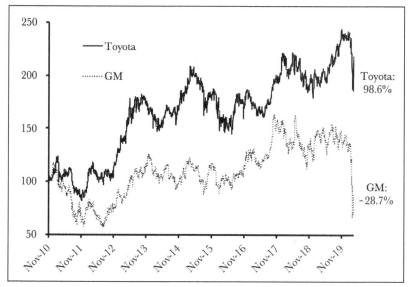

Rebased to 100 and adjusted for dividends.
Source: Bloomberg.

Total Return: BP vs Exxon (5 Year)

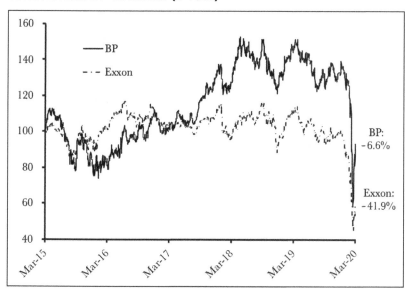

Rebased to 100 and adjusted for dividends.
Source: Bloomberg.

In our view, these examples are just the tip of the iceberg of a trend that will bifurcate valuations within many industries. With the daily drumbeat of bad news on climate, we feel this is an irreversible trend for the coming decade.

ACTIONS BY OVERLOOK

Overlook will continue our employee and company carbon offset programs and we will eliminate more selected industries going forward. We will also analyze our holdings consistent with the qualities of Solution companies, described above. To achieve cross-industry analysis in a consistent and integrated manner, we have allocated time of a dedicated research analyst, Angela Wang, to carry out the review. Angela works with each member of the Investment Team to carry out these detailed and technical reviews. Angela has become an expert in carbon accounting and other issues related to carbon emissions.

Each company in the portfolio receives an Environmental Score. In 2019, our first year of grading, fully 44% of our portfolio received failing Environmental Scores simply due to the inadequate disclosure of corporate emissions data. While we generally know the emissions of those 44% of our portfolio through competitor analysis, Asian corporates and Overlook's portfolio are lagging unacceptably behind their counterparts in the West. Much work is still to be carried out.

The rise of the ESG Movement has opened up opportunities for Overlook to address Asia's unsatisfactory results with a bigger stick. Starting in 2020, we will communicate the Environmental Scores to the Chairmen and CEOs of our portfolio companies privately and confidentially. These communications will utilize the same techniques that have made Modern Finance Technology successful over the past two decades. The letters will be private and confidential, fact-based, honest, detailed, and respectful. They will review current efforts and ask for specific actions. We acknowledge that Rome was not built in a day, but we do not have decades to waste.

BUT HERE'S THE GOOD NEWS

Over the past three years, we have seen specific examples in our portfolio holdings in which our private and confidential communications have accelerated the deployment of meaningful investment in climate change solutions. These actions confirm that the respective company is part of the solution and can be trusted to do more in the future. We believe that the recent rise of the ESG Movement will further amplify Overlook's voice. This excites us as investors.

CONCLUSION

My dad always told me the greatest thing about a career in investment management is that investors get to learn new things every day. Indeed, the environmental challenge we collectively confront today will give investors many new facts to learn and actions to take. Thankfully, at Overlook, we are not starting this journey today.

PART FIVE

The Poster Child

W E HAVE SAID in this book that prior to the 1997/98 Asian Crisis, fundamental investing was a challenge in Asia. Economies were developing so rapidly that corporate Asia pursued growth without regard to global best practices. Debt levels rose unsustainably, capital management became haphazard, and conflicts of interest dominated corporate governance. The painful lessons of the Asian Crisis triggered a watershed moment that enabled Asia's best companies to mature into disciplined, high-return businesses. These were Asia's New Winners; the superior companies that Overlook had always wanted to own.

It was at this time that Overlook first encountered Taiwan Semiconductor Manufacturing Company. TSMC ticked all the boxes as a Superior Business. Its business model was profitable and cash flow positive, and management was disciplined and talented. However, our enthusiasm was dampened because TSMC had a blind spot: its business practices did not deliver value to shareholders. Overlook's Modern Finance Technology helped TSMC unlock that missing piece.

It is a core theme of this book that investment firms and corporations must have profitable business models and effective business practices to achieve excellent performance and deliver that performance to investors and shareholders. This culminating chapter of *The Model* tells the story of Overlook's two-decade relationship with TSMC. It tells how the market cap of TSMC starts at a fraction of Intel's and ends at a multiple of Intel's. The success of the TSMC Model, in many ways, parallels the success of The Overlook Model. We grew and prospered together.

TSMC: Asia's Finest Public Company

As the world is no longer peaceful, TSMC is gaining vital importance in geostrategic terms.

— MORRIS CHANG,
Founder and Chairman of TSMC

I T IS INEVITABLE that a successful fund management company becomes closely associated with a company that has a superior business model. For my dad it was Automatic Data Processing; for Jon Bush it was Rite Aid. At Overlook, we can only dream of finding another company to rival our association with Taiwan Semiconductor Manufacturing Company (TSMC). When we talk at Overlook about companies that embrace the highest values of The Overlook Model, TSMC is our poster child.

Taiwan Semiconductor Manufacturing Company

In 1987, at the invitation of the Government of Taiwan, Dr. Morris Chang led the establishment of the world's first semiconductor foundry business model. For the past three decades, TSMC's business has accelerated the deployment of leading-edge technology throughout the world and has become the world's largest semiconductor foundry.

Fast-forward from the time of Overlook's first investment in TSMC in 2000. Who would have expected TSMC's market capitalization to be 2.5 times that of Intel's when it was only 14% of Intel's 20 years ago? Further, who would have conceived of the notion that TSMC's strategic role today in global chipmaking could either spark a war between the U.S. and China over Taiwan, or be the precise reason why Taiwan will avert a war?

This chapter is the story of TSMC: Asia's finest public company from the perspective of Overlook Investments, a 20-year shareholder.

The TSMC Model

Overlook's investors know that we first invested in TSMC over two decades ago. We have watched it grow from a US$ 28 billion market cap company in 2000, when we bought our first shares, into one of the top 11 public companies in the world today. The ride often felt breathtaking and jaw dropping.

The past 20 years have given us the time to recognize that TSMC's fundamental strengths emanate from the TSMC Model, described in detail below. This description of the five components of TSMC's Model could have been written in 2002 or last month. In fact, we struggle to find individual words, let alone sentences, in Overlook's 2012 description of the TSMC Model that we would change today. This highlights the power of TSMC's Model. It anchors and directs the corporation that operates in one of the fastest changing industries in the world.

Here is a revised summary of the components of the TSMC Model from our September 2012 report:

"WE DON'T COMPETE WITH OUR CUSTOMERS"

The first time I walked into TSMC's offices in 2001 in Hsinchu, Taiwan, I was told, "We don't compete with our customers." If I walk into TSMC's office today, I am still told, "We don't compete with our customers." Not competing with customers, which Intel and Samsung do, has allowed fabless integrated circuit (IC) design houses to disclose their intellectual property in confidence to TSMC.

This is a simple concept but central to the TSMC Model. It allows customers to have the confidence to expose their intellectual property (IP) and product designs to TSMC, so as to work in partnership with TSMC's own library of IP and manufacturing services to improve quality, timeliness, cost effectiveness of their product introductions, and the speed of migration to higher technology nodes. At a fundamental level, TSMC's Model helped customers lower the cost of innovation and become more successful.

SPREADING COST OF FAB OVER MANY CUSTOMERS

Morris Chang, TSMC's founder and CEO [he has since retired], developed a simple but revolutionary idea 25 years ago when he created the dedicated IC foundry business model. The goal was to offer cutting-edge semiconductor manufacturing capacity to fabless IC design houses that could not afford to load a semiconductor facility at a rate that would earn an economic return. By spreading the capital and R&D costs across multiple customers, TSMC achieves high utilization, high profitability, and more than an economic return. Since the founding of TSMC, the cost and size of semiconductor fabs have done nothing but rise. This, in turn, has driven larger and larger customers to TSMC's door. These trends have accelerated. Overlook is hard pressed to find a business with such a formidable barrier to entry.

TREATING EVERYONE THE SAME

We have a saying at Overlook that has been central to our Model: "One fund, no side accounts, no special deals, largest and smallest investors are always treated the same." So it is with TSMC in the sense that large customers do not get an unfair advantage over small start-ups. I imagine Morris Chang learned years ago that today's small companies might be tomorrow's behemoths, and those entrepreneurs will have long memories and genuine loyalty toward partners who help them achieve their early success.

INVESTMENT IN
CUTTING-EDGE TECHNOLOGY

It is an absolute necessity for large fabless design houses to have access to leading-edge manufacturing technology. TMSC knows this, but the challenge is double-edged. The good news is that if a foundry can provide leading-edge technology and manufacturing scale, its business will grow quickly and with high profitability. The bad news is that bringing online the latest technology at large scale is extremely expensive, both in terms of hardware to build the fabs and R&D expenses to develop the tools and manufacturing services. This combination of hardware and software is essential for the fab owner to migrate customers to the more advanced technology nodes that offer high manufacturing yields and profits. Just the R&D for perfecting the most advanced node costs approximately US$ 1.5 billion before any revenue is generated. [That figure has doubled to over US$ 3 billion today.] This R&D cost is fully expensed by TSMC. TSMC's record of bringing online leading-edge technology is unparalleled.

ADHERING TO A DISCIPLINED FINANCIAL MODEL

TSMC has four main financial goals targeted for achievement across the full cycle, not just each year [bracketed figures are as of 2021]:

1. 20% return on equity [more than 25% today].

2. 10% E.P.S. growth [10–15% today].

3. NT$ 3.00 per share cash dividend [> NT$ 11.00 dividend].

4. Discipline in pricing its products to achieve self-financed growth.

These simple financial targets massively understate the sophistication of TSMC's financial model, which incorporates and integrates a large, but publicly undefined, number of indicators that have proven over the years to deliver the goals. From 2007 to 2020, the return on average equity has averaged 23.9%, E.P.S. has grown at a compound rate of 15.7%, and the company has been consistently cash flow positive despite spending US$ 149 billion in capex and paying just short of US$ 70 billion in dividends over these 14 years. Not bad for a company that in 2007 had an average market capitalization of US$ 53 billion.

TSMC: A McCoy Becomes The Real McCoy

We first invested in TSMC over 20 years ago and it was not all rosy from the start. Intel had a seemingly insurmountable technology lead and a market capitalization seven times that of TSMC; United Microelectronics Corporation (UMC) was a formidable competitor in Taiwan; and TSMC followed corporate governance and capital management policies that disadvantaged minority shareholders and limited the return on equity to 11% in 2003. In short, TSMC had a blind spot in their Model.

In 2004, as I readied to sell our shares, I sent a personal letter to Dr.

Morris Chang, then Chairman and CEO of TSMC, the father of the Asian electronics industry and one of the greatest executives Overlook has known in Asia. This is the story, from our December 2004 report, when Morris was not yet Morris:

In July 2004 I wrote to Dr. Morris Chang about my concerns over the corporate governance of TSMC. I set out four actions that I felt TSMC needed to embrace to reverse this situation. I expected little more than a pat reply as so often comes when I write to CEOs to challenge the status quo. To my surprise, however, Dr. Chang circulated the letter to senior management, members of the board of directors, and representatives of the Government of Taiwan, who he told me were not happy with the criticism.

And then he called me directly – not the CFO, not the head of Investor Relations, not his secretary, but Morris personally. Over the past five months, I have engaged in active debate with Dr. Chang and senior management over TSMC's corporate governance policies, or more specifically: their cash dividend policy; their history of favoring share buybacks over cash dividends; their policy of giving free shares to employees; and their history of giving preference to major shareholders in the sale of ADRs in New York at a premium.

I am delighted to report that in early November 2004, TSMC called an extraordinary general meeting of shareholders and subsequently removed a restrictive clause limiting cash dividends from their articles of association. At the same time TSMC also announced that cash dividends would be given priority over share buybacks.

While I suspect Overlook was not the only voice calling for change at TSMC, my interactions with Dr. Chang and the senior management, and TSMC's announcements, leave me in little doubt that tiny Overlook, with $ 285 million of assets under management, did have an impact on accelerating important change at TSMC, which had a market capitalization of US$ 37 billion at that time. I believe that Overlook's persistence and clear stand made the directors and management realize that maintaining the status quo was not a viable option.

What gives us the edge in such situations is Overlook's unique position of being an informed, engaged, and long-term shareholder. This provides us with opportunities to alter the direction of corporations, especially ones with honest and insightful management such as that of Dr. Chang and his colleagues at TSMC.

Our efforts to help TSMC remove a blind spot in their business practices showed Overlook that MFT's time had arrived. When the increase in returns and duration justify our work on MFT, Overlook feels more confident than ever that we can remove blind spots from superior companies and help build better companies.

Overlook Welcomes Dr. Chang and Dr. Sun to the Overlook Hall of Fame

In 2006 it gave us particular satisfaction to name Morris to the Overlook Hall of Fame. Belatedly, we named Dr. Elizabeth Sun, one of Overlook's all-time favorite corporate executives, to the Hall of Fame in 2019. Elizabeth was instrumental in implementing the new business practices at TSMC in 2004/05.

Dr. Morris Chang's 2006 induction to the Overlook Hall of Fame:

> I am pleased to name Dr. Morris Chang as the 12th member of the Overlook Hall of Fame. Dr. Chang is Chairman and Founder of Taiwan Semiconductor Manufacturing Company (TSMC) and an executive whom I consider to be the father of the electronics industry in Asia. Nearly every technology company we visit in Taiwan or China owes its success at some level to TSMC and Morris Chang. Dr. Chang was among the first executives to embrace the core components of Overlook's Modern Finance Technology. He listened to us. His commitment to high corporate governance standards

resulted in the payment of the largest cash dividend in the history of Taiwan in 2005.

I feel privileged that Overlook has worked with Dr. Chang in helping TSMC become a better corporation and am honored to name him a member of the Overlook Hall of Fame.

Dr. Elizabeth Sun's 2019 induction to the Overlook Hall of Fame:

> Overlook's holding of TSMC has nearly perfectly overlapped with Elizabeth's 17-year tenure at TSMC, and her retirement is a bittersweet moment as we have appreciated our successful relationship for so many years. Throughout her career Elizabeth has been a vigorous and influential voice among the senior leadership at TSMC on the critical issues of corporate governance, capital management, and creating a true partnership between management and shareholders. Elizabeth has a unique ability to toggle seamlessly between answering complex technical questions about the manufacture of advanced semiconductor chips and reviewing the components of TSMC's sophisticated pricing and capital management models. Over the last two decades it has been our honor to watch TSMC develop into the highest quality company in Asia. Overlook owes Elizabeth an enormous debt of gratitude for her contribution to TSMC and Overlook.

Warren Buffett

As TSMC implemented the changes in corporate governance and capital management, we wrote to update Overlook's investors:

In Q3 2007, TSMC's share price was sold off from NT$ 69.4 to NT$ 36.8 under pressure from investors discounting a recession in the U.S. At the lows of late November, TSMC was an exceptional buy in the great tradition of value investing. On November 27, 2007, I took the opportunity to fulfill a personal ambition of mine by recommending TSMC to Warren Buffett of Berkshire Hathaway. I had no expectation that Mr. Buffett would buy the stock, for a host of reasons, but the process of writing the letter reaffirmed Overlook's conviction that TSMC was a great stock for us to own. Rather than paraphrase our letter, I have copied excerpts from it below. I think these comments serve to outline why Overlook still owns TSMC.

EXCERPTS FROM LETTER TO WARREN BUFFETT FROM RICHARD LAWRENCE, DATED NOVEMBER 27, 2007.

Dear Mr. Buffett,

I recommend that you consider an investment in Taiwan Semiconductor Manufacturing Company (TSMC).

After 23 years of following the investment philosophies of Berkshire Hathaway, it gives me great pleasure that I have an investment idea that may be of interest to you. I hope that this idea will at least partly repay you for your contribution to my development as an investor.

As background, I am a 51-year-old American who moved to Hong Kong in 1985. For the last 22 years I have been investing in the public stock markets of Asia and for the past 16 years I have run a modestly sized, value-oriented partnership that has generated returns of 14.3% per year. Much of what I do is founded on the business and investment philosophies of Berkshire Hathaway and the value investing community.

TSMC has the following attributes that may be worthy of your attention:

- Dominant market share
- Strong pricing power indicated by high and steady profit margins
- Substantial amounts of free cash flow
- Rising capital efficiency and returns on investment

- Bargain valuation

- Ethical management

VALUE PROPOSITION OFFERED BY TSMC

DOMINANT MARKET SHARE

Over the past five years TSMC has generated 60% of the foundry industry's revenue, 64% of the industry's operating cash flow, and 103% of the industry's operating profits adjusted for full employee costs, while spending just 49% of the industry's R&D. As a result, TSMC's lead over competitors is even wider in the most sophisticated products that naturally carry higher growth, wider margins and higher barrier to entry. This commanding position underpins a virtuous cycle for TSMC and a vicious cycle for competitors who are falling further and further behind TSMC's productivity and advanced manufacturing techniques.

Rarely have I seen an industry where the leading player captures so much of the value.

STRONG PRICING POWER INDICATED BY HIGH AND STEADY PROFIT MARGINS

Mr. Buffett, you have taught me that most high-quality companies have strong pricing power. I understand this to be reflected in high absolute profit margins matched with low volatility.

Over the past ten years, TSMC has generated the highest cash gross profit margins (71.4%) and the lowest annual volatility of cash gross profit margin of any company in our portfolio. To put these numbers in a wider perspective, TSMC's pricing power (as calculated by Overlook) compares favorably with 10-year figures from Coca-Cola, Johnson & Johnson, The Washington Post Company and Gillette (until its merger). I think these figures confirm that TSMC has substantial pricing power and that the Company's fabs generate high value-added for its customers.

Certainly, these results are not what we might expect from a typical manufacturing company.

SUBSTANTIAL AMOUNTS OF FREE CASH FLOW

For the past 10 years, cash flow before capex has averaged 59.25% of TSMC's revenue. In the early days of TSMC, when revenue compounded at 25% per annum, the company used its cash flow to pay for multi-billion-dollar manufacturing facilities. However, since 2002 there has been a clearly visible trend towards declining capital intensity of the business. Capex as a percentage of cash flow has averaged only 46.2% over the past five years against an average of 125.9% in the preceding five years. The drop in capital intensity is supported by slower industry growth and maintenance capex that equals only 10–15% of annual capex.

As a result of this high-quality cash flow, TSMC's cash, dividends and stock buybacks have ballooned and should stay very healthy.

RISING CAPITAL EFFICIENCY AND RETURNS ON INVESTMENT

On the back of falling capital intensity and higher asset turnover ratios, TSMC has initiated a process of implementing an efficient capital structure. In 2004 the company declared its first cash dividend and in 2005 increased the dividend payout ratio to 67%. In November 2007 TSMC announced an immediate US$ 1.5 billion share buyback to be completed by February 2008 and its intention to initiate three further buybacks of US$ 1.0 billion per year in 2008, 2009 and 2010.

These steps will raise the return on average equity from 11.1% in 2003 to above 30% by 2009. TSMC's return on average operating net assets should top 50% by 2009, leaving room for TSMC's return on equity to rise further. However, despite efforts to improve the capital structure, net cash has still risen from 16% of shareholders' equity in 2002 to an estimated 23% in December 2007.

I believe TSMC's share is a bargain in the best tradition of value investing, especially for a US$ 50 billion company. TSMC is currently trading at between 8.5x and 9.0x owners' earnings. From my estimate of between US$ 5.0 and US$ 5.5 billion of owners' earnings, TSMC is able to reinvest US$ 2.0 billion in the business at an unlevered rate of return of between 15% and 20%. I expect the rest will be distributed to shareholders generating a 5–6% dividend yield. Furthermore, investment returns for shareholders will be enhanced by share buybacks that will lower excess cash reserves and enhance E.P.S. growth rates.

ETHICAL MANAGEMENT

I consider Dr. Morris Chang, Chairman and Founder of TSMC, to be an ethical and honest business leader. In 1987 he resigned from Texas Instruments, returned to Taiwan to set up TSMC and, in doing so, became the "father" of the Asian electronics industry.

[We described for Mr. Buffett our interactions with Morris Chang earlier in this chapter.]

TSMC's Model vs. TSMC's Results

In retrospect, my letter to Warren Buffett was deficient. The letter describes in comprehensive detail the results of TSMC. It does not define the components of the TSMC Model, nor does it explain that TSMC's results occurred due to the execution of their Model. It is TSMC's Model that drives the results, not vice versa. Our letter to Mr. Buffett neglected to explain the source of TSMC's enduring strengths and therefore, we are partly responsible for Berkshire missing out on a 24.8% IRR over nearly 14 years.

Don't compete with customers, treat all customers the same, spread the cost of the fabs over many customers... The components of the TSMC Model are the drivers of TSMC's success. The TSMC story is, in many ways, similar to other companies we have highlighted in this book that had superior businesses and aligned business practices. It is also similar to Overlook's story. Our Investment Philosophy has generated outperformance over the universe and our commitment to the Overlook Business Practices has enabled us to deliver outperformance to the investors. The 14.3% return and the 6.5 percentage points of outperformance are the results that arise from the execution of The Overlook Model, not vice versa. There is no other logical explanation.

For 20 years Overlook's investment in TSMC generated capital-weighted returns of 18.1%. We consider ourselves fortunate that Morris Chang picked up the phone 17 years ago in reply to Overlook's letter and asked us to work with TSMC to resolve our differences. At that moment Overlook understood that TSMC was the finest public company in Asia.

Conclusion:
Don't Mess with The Model

Just one more thing…

At the inception of this book we posed two questions:

1. How did Overlook achieve its success?

2. How can Overlook best ensure future success?

To answer the first question, I quote a line from earlier in the book.

We grew at 14.3% for three decades. We outperformed the universe by 6.5 percentage points per year for 30 years. More importantly, we delivered 14.2% returns to the Overlook investors. We outperformed when we were a small fund, we outperformed when we were a mid-sized fund, and we continue to outperform as a large fund. We outperformed when I made every stock pick and we have continued to outperform now that I make almost none of the stock picks.

The only logical and believable explanation is that Overlook's success was generated by the consistent execution of The Overlook Model, and this gives us confidence about the future.

Throughout the book we described the components of The Overlook Model. We explained how the Investment Philosophy, supported by detailed financial analysis, pushes the portfolio to the top of the Pyramid; and how, if this position can be maintained for five years, the portfolio is well placed for outperformance above the universe. We also articulated our commitment to the Overlook Business Practices, particularly the legal Cap on Subscriptions, which can nearly guarantee the delivery of the outperformance to investors. The failure to combine superior businesses and conflict-free business practices reduces the ability to achieve superior returns.

We showed how Overlook seeks to invest in companies with superior businesses and business practices that create long-duration value for shareholders. As is the case with investment managers, a company is not able to deliver value to shareholders unless it can combine superior business characteristics with appropriate business practices. And we shared many case studies of Overlook's successes and failures.

Superior businesses with aligned business practices have generated Overlook's returns. We owe gratitude to great companies like TSMC, CP All, Kingboard Chemical, NetEase, Café de Coral, and ThaiRe; and exceptional executives like Morris Chang, Khun Dhanin, Paul Cheung, Patrick Chan, William Ding, Michael Chan, and Khun Surachai.

To answer the second question, our collective optimism at Overlook is based on a number of fundamental factors that are embedded in The Overlook Model.

- We have a transition plan that takes into consideration the second, third, and even fourth generation of leaders at Overlook.

- We have a team of individuals that embrace diversity yet remain grounded in teamwork. We win and lose together.

- We have an equity analysis discipline grounded in the core components of the Overlook Investment Philosophy. We appreciate nothing more than a well-considered investment thesis or a well-designed spreadsheet that identifies drivers and risks.

- We have established Business Practices formed around our goal of delivering returns to investors.

- We have confidence in The Overlook Model from knowledge that we have withstood so many challenges in the past.

- We have watched The Model evolve, grow, embrace new features, face new challenges, but never be abandoned. Change is our constant; The Model is our rock.

The future will bring change: both bull markets and bear markets, some good stocks and some mistakes, and at times, a change of some faces. If we continue to execute The Overlook Model, we like our chances.

The Value of
Bear Markets

Contributed by Marc Faber

Biography of Marc Faber

Dr. Marc Faber was Overlook's first friend, having generously allowed me to work in his spare office when I was conceptualizing Overlook in 1991. Over the years Marc kindly included various pieces from Overlook in his acclaimed newsletter, *The Gloom, Boom & Doom Report*, so it gives me particular joy to include Marc's piece on bear markets in *The Model*. Marc is one of the most astute and prolific commentators on financial markets in the world today. His writings have left an indelible mark on Overlook and I am forever thankful for his contributions. This piece gives a glimpse into Marc's unique historical perspective on bear markets. I hope you enjoy this as much as I did.

The Value of Bear Markets

I T SHOULD NOT be surprising that investors have become accustomed to stock bull markets since equity prices have tended to move up, albeit irregularly, since the last major inflation-adjusted low in 1982, when the Dow Jones Industrial briefly traded below 800.

The commonality of all bull markets is that they develop some leadership among stocks or sectors. In the 1970 to 1973 bull market, the leadership was concentrated among "quality growth stocks" (the nifty-fifty); in the 1974 to 1980 bull market, the leadership consisted of mining companies, and oil and energy-related stocks; and in the 1994 to 2000 bull market, investors focused on the technology, media, and telecommunication (TMT) sectors – just to name a few examples.

Another characteristic of bull markets that have a concentrated leadership among selected sectors is that they inevitably lead to some sort of "bubble" or "investment mania." The late financial historian Charles Kindleberger wrote that, "the word *mania...* connotes a loss of touch with reality or rationality, even something close to mass hysteria or insanity."

The beauty about this most speculative phase of the bull market is that it creates a poor allocation of capital. Performance-hungry investors and short-term speculators' funds flow into the "bubble" sectors because that is where the upside action takes place. This speculative phase is accompanied by the media's captivation with "new era" stocks and a massive increase in new issues related to the subject of speculation. For the *value* investor this is the most painful but also the most interesting phase of bull markets. Why? Painful it is, because value investors will all underperform the soaring stock market, which is driven by a narrow leadership. Interesting it is, because all the world's money flows into the *boom* sectors and, therefore, completely neglects other sectors of the economy. Economists call this phenomenon *misallocation of capital* and Walter Bagehot observed in his essay on the historian Edward Gibbon that, "Much has been written about panics and manias, much more than with the most outstretched intellect we are able to follow or conceive; but one thing is certain, that at particular times a great deal of stupid people have a great deal of stupid money."

Now, thanks to the "great deal of stupid money" in the hands of "a great deal of stupid people" the undervaluation of the neglected sectors or countries reaches extremes that provide the *patient* and *disciplined* investor "a great deal of lifetime investment opportunities."

The way night follows day, investment manias are followed by severe bear markets (certainly in real terms), during which the bubble sectors get annihilated. Now, I am the first person to agree with the late Leon Levy who expressed the view that, "For most people, the most dangerous self-delusion is that even a falling market will not affect their stocks, which they bought out of a canny understanding of value." However, we need to realize that a neglected stock or a neglected sector, which by definition becomes attractively valued, is also very illiquid. This is so because during the time this sector has become unpopular it moved from weak holders into strong hands, and insiders and deep-value investors who will only be prepared to part with their holdings at much higher prices.

A manic peak in stocks will in the inevitable subsequent bear market lead to a *change* in leadership because, as an old Chinese proverb says, "When the wall starts collapsing, 10,000 people rush to push it down." And, therefore, the "great deal of stupid money" in the hands of "a great deal of stupid people" rushes out of the object of speculation and looks for new opportunities elsewhere within the markets.

I believe, having been an investor in Overlook since its foundation in 1991, that the shepherds of our funds, my dear friend Richard Lawrence and his highly capable team, understand the importance of bear markets in shifting money out of overvalued sectors of markets into sectors and stocks where most people would shake their heads because they cannot see why anyone would touch such a country, commodity, stock, property, bond, etc., even with a ten-foot pole.

I am not exaggerating when I say that the performance of the Overlook team has been outstanding over the last 30 years. Will it continue? I have high confidence in The Overlook Model because it combines *integrity* (aligning the client's interest with their own), *courage* (taking large, concentrated positions in attractively priced companies after extensive analysis), *patience* (all investors say they are patient until a 10% decline in the value of their investments turns them into impatient nervous wrecks), and *discipline* (having power over your mind, which lets you find strength and excellence).

It has been a very rewarding experience in my life to meet Richard in the mid-1980s, after he had just arrived in Hong Kong and see him start Overlook with very little capital and amidst humble beginnings, and grow his fund to a large size mostly through capital gains with impeccable integrity, and at the same time building an excellent team of professionals.

From my heart I can say "Happy Birthday" to Overlook Investments and stay the course.

Acknowledgments

The celebration of Overlook's 30th anniversary is a celebration of Overlook's investors. I apologize that we have not mentioned the names of the investors who have supported us for decades. Creating direct bonds with investors has given meaning to our work, but we simply have too many great relationships to mention names in this book. Our investor base, with their long-term outlook, has allowed the Investment Philosophy and Business Practices to create the Overlook Margin of Safety.

I am delighted *The Model* gave me an opportunity to acknowledge the contributions of so many corporate executives to Overlook's success. We have been blessed to interact with so many talented leaders. I apologize to the vast number of Asian executives who have contributed to Overlook's success but are not mentioned in *The Model*.

Writing a book is more challenging and time consuming than I imagined as I sat on a beach in Hawaii over Christmas 2020. The experience was made gratifying by the support and encouragement of my family: my wife Dee, who never rolled her eyes even when I knew she wanted to; my brothers, Jim and Philip Lawrence, whose guidance, insights, and constant good humor helped me to navigate a new challenge; my children, Skye and Blake, and their spouses-to-be, Seth and Dina, who provided confidence that I could get this finished. And of course, my mother, Starr, who simply delighted in the idea that I could actually write a book after my checkered early education.

The Model has given James Squire, Leonie Foong, William Leung, Alan Morgan and me an opportunity to provide the most detailed explanation to date of The Overlook Model. I wish to thank all my colleagues at Overlook and their families for their improvements to *The Model* and dedication to Overlook. Jason Lin gets a special thanks for his work creating the Margin of Safety equations that I love, yet readily admit are indecipherable to most humans.

I would like to thank Jim Hackett, Esther Adams and Craig Pearce and his team at Harriman House for their support in creating The Model. I have known Jim to be a great writer for nearly five decades and it gives me great joy to be the first to put his name on the cover of a book. Jim has known Overlook since inception, so he was uniquely qualified to help bring clarity to the stories and the theories that comprise the book. Esther has been my right hand for over 15 years. I have maintained for many years that she could be the assistant for the chairmen of the largest companies on Earth but somehow I was lucky to have employed her. Craig Pearce, my editor, and his colleagues at Harriman House were the perfect folks to help me execute this book. Craig could have buried me in edits, yet he hit the mark every time, both demanding excellence and allowing the book to be mine. It was a wonderful experience. The Model would not have happened without Esther, Jim and Craig.

I am thankful for the contributions from a whole host of mentors who sadly are not here to understand their impact on me, including Richard Lawrence, George Bartlett, Jonathan Bush, Barry Metzger, Leon Levy and David Swensen. And to the mentors and supporters who happily are still hanging around: including Doña Emilia Mendoza and her colleagues at Proyecto Mirador, Jeremy Grantham and his cast of the usual suspects, RC w/ DP, the folks at Cool Effect and High Tide Foundation, Ellen and Jon Zinke, Mimi and Peabody Hutton, Tim Noonan, the indomitable Dr. Marc Faber and all my friends who enrich my life.

I am gratefully indebted as well to the people who willingly responded when asked for their help. The members of Overlook's Board of Advisors:

Terry Fok, David Halperin, Michael Lonergan, and Aubrey Li; Cheah Cheng-hye, V. Prem Watsa, Ted Seides, Antonio Foglia, Paula Volent, David Patterson, Crosby Smith, Jim Ruddy, Ming Chang, Mike Lonergan, Desmond Kinch, Charles and Louis Gave, Khun Surachai Sirivallop, Eric Sandlund, Jan Greer, Peter Simon, and Dr. Elizabeth Sun. All helped shape Overlook and *The Model*.

And finally, I wish to express my admiration and appreciation to the people of Hong Kong who accepted this New Yorker along with his wife with open arms when we arrived in 1985 with two backpacks and no money. Their energy and entrepreneurial zeal opened my eyes and gave me the second home that made Overlook possible.

Index